Praise for *The AI MD*™ *Rx* and Dr. Hamed Abbaszadegan

As a practicing cardiologist, I encounter patients collecting biometrics more frequently than any other specialty on a daily basis. Patients are gaining access to large data via fast developing technology and are weaponized by this data when visiting and discussing preventive and therapeutic strategies at the doctors' offices and hospitals. It is imperative for us clinicians to understand what the pattern recognition tools are capable of and help our patients decipher through the data points and reach a meaningful understanding too. This book is noble in its kind as it redefines the AI in medicine concept and dissects the topic so we can decide what matters. It guides us to untangle the ambiguities associated with the massive flow of data.

- David Biglari, DO, PhD, FACC, FSCAI
Cardiologist

With clarity and authority, *The AI MD™ Rx* redefines how technology can empower individuals to track, understand, and protect their health long before disease develops. This book guides the needs of modern medicine: a credible and practical roadmap for using AI and wearables to shift from reactive care to true prevention enhancing patient outcomes and advancing the future of therapeutics. As the old adage goes "an ounce of prevention is worth a pound of cure," *The AI MD™ Rx* provides a pathway for a systematically efficient and effective healthcare model for the future."

- Samir Sultan, DO
Pulmonologist

As a psychiatrist, I see it constantly – wearables designed to empower have become a source of anxiety, perfectionism, and mental overload. More data does not necessarily mean more peace of mind. *The AI MD™ Rx* gets this right. It gives readers the psychological framework to transform health data from a trigger into a tool – building clarity, confidence, and a healthier relationship with themselves.

- Mona Amini, MD, MBA
Psychiatrist

The AI MD™ Rx isn't just information, it is a blueprint. If you want to look better, move better, and perform at your highest level, this book makes health optimization simple, actionable, and built for real results.

- Devonte Woods
Personal Trainer

What I appreciate about *The AI MD™ Rx* is it speaks to something many of us feel but have not yet defined. We are surrounded by more health information than ever, yet we often feel less certain about what it all means. Dr. Hamed Abbaszadegan brings clarity, calm, and wisdom to that uncertainty. This book feels both timely and deeply human, helping readers see how technology can become a motivator and guide instead of a burden. This is not only timely, but necessary. We are seeing an entirely new opportunity to integrate care and technology. *The AI MD™ Rx* is the beginning.

- Don Taylor
Director, Alliance for Physician Leadership, UT Dallas
Professor of Practice

In an era when healthcare technology is advancing faster than most clinicians and patients can reasonably absorb, Dr. Hamed Abbaszadegan brings rare clarity, credibility, and practical authority to the conversation. As a physician, healthcare executive, and clinical informaticist, he has the uncommon ability to command a highly complex technological landscape while translating it into guidance that is precise, actionable, and grounded in real-world care. *The AI MD™ Rx* arrives at a pivotal moment, establishing a much-needed foundation for a more intuitive, data-driven approach to health and well-being that is accessible not only to clinicians, but to the everyday patient navigating an increasingly complex system. He is leading this field in the way it should be led: as a physician first, with the judgment, discipline, and perspective required to help healthcare adopt innovation responsibly.

- Omesh Singh, DO, MBA, MS, FACOI
Internal Medicine Physician and Healthcare Executive

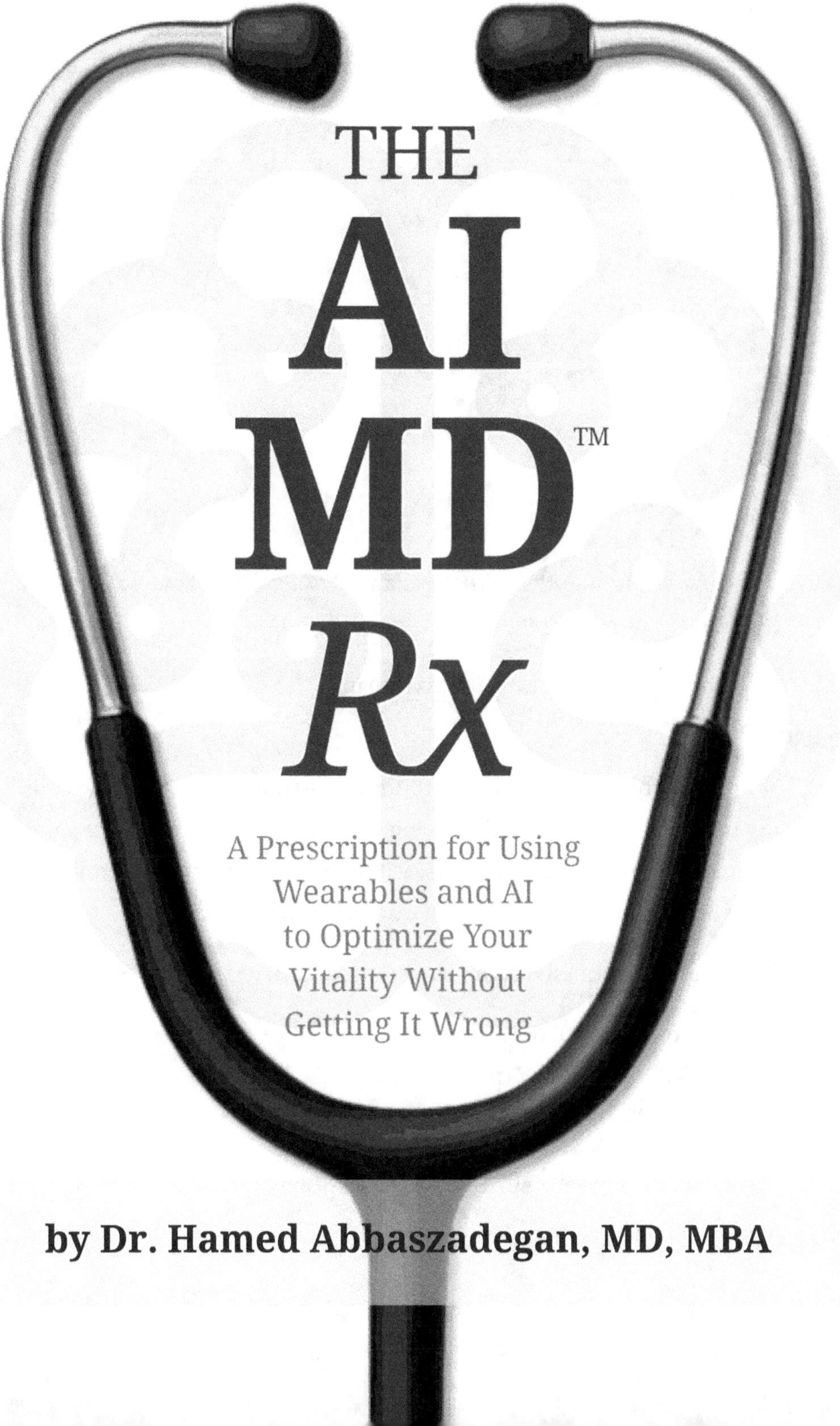

THE AI MD™ *Rx*

A Prescription for Using Wearables and AI to Optimize Your Vitality Without Getting It Wrong

by Dr. Hamed Abbaszadegan, MD, MBA

The AI MD™ Rx:
A Prescription for Using Wearables and AI to Optimize Your Vitality Without Getting It Wrong

First Edition: May 2026
ISBN 979-8-9955936-0-7 (paperback)
ISBN 979-8-9955936-1-4 (ebook)

Printed in the United States of America

Published by Rising Icon

To my wife

You have unlocked my true potential. Your unwavering patience has always stemmed from love. I dedicate this book to you, my true soul mate and partner.

Hamed Abbaszadegan, MD, MBA

The AI MD™

> ***This book is my gift to all as we all deserve the insight and strategies to living well.***

Dr. Hamed Abbaszadegan is a physician executive and clinical informaticist helping people and health systems turn data into better decision making. He specializes in translating wearable signals into practical decision rules that drive measurable improvements in energy, performance, and long-term health.

Double board-certified in Internal Medicine and Clinical Informatics, Dr. Abbaszadegan has spent over a decade building real-world clinical decision support and responsible AI that fits how humans actually work at the bedside and beyond.

He chaired a national committee that developed and published AI Governance in Healthcare Operations as an American National Standard. This standard focused on ensuring AI tools enhance safety, usability, and outcomes.

As a committed educator, he has led clinical informatics training and teaches physician leadership, while remaining clinically active and mentoring the next generation of physicians.

Through The AI MD™ platform, he is building a wearables-first education community and biosimulation driven tools that empower individuals to experiment intelligently, adapt faster, and personalize their path towards longevity.

Contents

CHAPTER 1

Artificial Clarity

Cutting Through the Noise in the Era of AI Health Tech

The Age of Too Much Knowing

When I walk onto a stage and look out at the sea of faces, I can almost guess how many of you are wearing something that's watching you. Maybe it's a ring that measures your sleep, a band that tracks your heart rate, or a watch that congratulates you for standing up. Nearly all of us, in one form or another, are connected to a constant stream of biometric feedback.

We live in an era where we know more numbers about ourselves than at any point in human history, and yet, paradoxically, we understand ourselves less.

That's the irony of modern health: abundance has replaced clarity. You can scroll through your apps right now and find steps, calories, oxygen saturation, temperature, heart rate variability, recovery time, and a half-dozen metrics invented to make you feel like progress has a dashboard. But for most people, those dashboards create more questions than answers. Did I really sleep well? Why is my recovery lower today? What does "strain" actually mean? We've traded one form of uncertainty for another.

As a physician, I see it all the time. Patients walk into clinics clutching screenshots, spreadsheets, and anxiety. They've done the work, they're trying to be proactive, and yet they're exhausted by interpretation. They're living inside a kind of digital fog where data is plentiful but direction is missing. This is the world that gave birth to The AI MD™. You don't need another device or another app. You require a framework to give you a way to reclaim understanding in a world drowning in information.

What AI Really Means

Before we go further, let's reset what "AI" actually is, because the term has been hijacked by marketing. Artificial Intelligence isn't magic, and it isn't replacing doctors. At its core, AI is pattern recognition at scale. Feed it enough data, and it starts noticing relationships that human eyes miss. Finding relationships in data can lead to reasoning that ultimately can create new guidance specific to you. There's a catch though, it doesn't know what matters until we tell it.

In medicine, that means AI can't replace clinical judgment; it can only amplify it. It's the assistant in the room, not the authority. Think of it like having an extra brain that never sleeps, cross-checking every lab value, trend, and prior note. That's the sweet spot: the partnership between data and discernment. AI will not replace doctors. However, the doctors who use AI will replace the doctors who don't.

Let's use a simple analogy: imagine C-3PO from Star Wars. He is polite, efficient, and fluent in millions of forms of communication. He's brilliant at translating, but he still needs direction from Luke. AI is the same. It translates chaos into patterns, but you still (and always will) decide what matters.

When we apply that idea to personal health, a similar truth emerges. Your wearable isn't your physician, it's your translator. It tells you what it sees, but not directly what it means. It will give you insights, scores and numbers presented to you, but where is the meaning if you do not feel any different? That is the missing bridge. It's the gap of space between data and decision. That's where most people get lost, and that's exactly where The AI MD™ lives.

The Illusion of Progress

Today there are over 350,000 health-related apps and devices on the market. They promise optimization, longevity, energy, clarity, and even youth. Yet the global rates of metabolic disease, burnout, anxiety, and insomnia continue to rise. That's not a random failure of effort, but rather a failure of integration.

Data without direction becomes noise. Metrics without meaning become marketing and when we confuse tracking with transformation, we create what I call the illusion of progress.

Let me give you a story. A patient I'll call Mark came to me with every possible gadget, two wearables, continuous glucose monitor, and a fridge full of supplements that looked like a chemistry set. He was spending nearly two hours a day tracking, logging, analyzing, and comparing. When I asked how he felt, he hesitated and said, "Honestly, I don't know anymore." That sentence hit me hard. How could someone measure everything and still feel uncertain? Was this just another case of hypochondria or a genuine effort to be in the best health possible? In my mind, I compared him to individuals who go to the gym frequently, but do not produce visible results. Effort without intention and proper understanding frequently yields no results. Guidance and use of evidence based practice will set him on the right path.

As information does not automatically equal improvement, without interpretation, even the best data just magnifies confusion. Mark didn't need more metrics, he needed a map.

That's what we're building with this book. A map that organizes data around meaningful decisions. A system that replaces guessing with guidance. Real progress isn't in the numbers, it's in what the numbers empower you to do next.

From Confusion to Clarity

So let's get practical. The first promise of The AI MD™ is Artificial Clarity, not artificial intelligence replacing you, but amplifying you. It's the process of turning complexity into clarity. To do that, we follow a structure every clinician knows instinctively: Assess. Align. Activate.

It's the same logic we use in medicine. We assess the situation, align on a plan, and activate treatment. You can apply the same model to your own body and technology.

In the chapters ahead, you'll learn how to:

- Assess your true goals before buying another device.
- Align your behaviors with data that actually matters.
- Activate consistent actions that create measurable, lasting results.

Before we go there, I want to leave you with this thought:

Health shouldn't feel like hacking. It should feel like understanding.

Artificial Clarity isn't about having more numbers or fewer numbers; it's about having the right meaning behind them. When meaning returns, momentum follows. That's when technology stops controlling your behavior, and starts supporting it.

The Bridge Between Data and Decision

When people first hear "AI MD," they assume it's a gadget, an app, or some expensive futuristic platform. That's not what this is. It's a philosophy wrapped in a framework, and it began as a reaction to chaos.

A few years ago, I noticed the same pattern repeating with almost every patient, entrepreneur, or executive I worked with. They were proactive, motivated, and educated. They owned every new device that promised optimization. Yet their energy was unpredictable, their recovery inconsistent, and their stress unexplainable.

The pattern wasn't in their physiology, it was in their process. They were tracking without translating.

Think about that for a second. If you track 30 data points but only understand three, you've created 27 points of confusion. That's a new form of overwhelm disguised as diligence that prevents you from maximizing actual progress.

From Numbers to Narratives

The human brain doesn't think in numbers; it thinks in stories. A good clinician doesn't just read your bloodwork, they translate it into a narrative: "This is what's happening inside you, and here's how to respond." That's what AI should do, and what The AI MD™ was designed to make possible for everyone, not just those in a hospital system.

We don't need more data. We need context, correlation, and coherence so we access the ability to connect what we see to what we feel.

So if your wearable says your recovery score is 63 today, what does that mean for your meeting at 9 a.m.? If your heart rate variability drops, does that mean skip the gym or meditate first? Without interpretation, every metric becomes a coin flip. With interpretation, it becomes a compass.

The Clinical Informaticist's Lens

In my field of Clinical Informatics, we live at the intersection of data, healthcare, human decision-making, and technology. Our goal isn't to collect more information; it's to *curate meaning*. That's the difference between an algorithm and an ally.

Artificial intelligence can analyze millions of data points in seconds, but only human intelligence can define what matters to *you*. Your health isn't a spreadsheet; it's a system of stories, behaviors, and feedback loops. The AI MD™ exists to unify those threads into a single, adaptive feedback system, a modern version of how great physicians used to practice medicine before it became fragmented.

Doctors used to know their patients so well they could sense when something was off long before labs confirmed it. The AI MD™ simply gives that intuition data-driven reinforcement, a 21st-century stethoscope for your entire life.

Case Study: When Numbers Don't Add Up

Take Erin, a 42 year old tech founder I worked with recently. She was averaging 12-hour days, managing a team across three time zones, and convinced that more tracking equaled more control. Every morning, she woke up to five notifications: sleep efficiency, readiness, glucose variability, recovery index, and strain score. Each metric told a different story, and every story contradicted the other.

When I asked what she did with the information, she said,

"Honestly, I just worry about it."

That's the modern symptom of the quantified self, data-driven anxiety. What she needed most was alignment, not another app. Once we stripped back the noise and focused on her Baseline Health Indicators (BHI): activity, heart rate variability (HRV), and sleep. That's when we finally saw the pattern.

Her activity was strong, her sleep adequate, but her HRV was flat. This pattern showed her body was over-trained and under-recovered. A simple adjustment, three days of intermittent grounding breathwork and reduced intensity, spiked her HRV by 20 points and transformed her clarity. The numbers didn't heal her. Understanding them did.

That's Artificial Clarity in action: turning overwhelming information into a simple, corrective insight. If you were wondering how such a simple adjustment can change HRV, grounding breathwork with a reduction in physical intensity can increase HRV through enhancing vagal activity and baroreflex sensitivity. Such techniques will be reviewed in more depth as we progress through the book.

The Baseline Health Indicator (BHI)

At the heart of this framework lies one of the most important concepts in this book: your BHI, which is short for Baseline Health Indicator.

It's the trifecta of metrics that govern nearly every system in the human body:

1. **Activity**: How much energy you expend.
2. **HRV** (Heart Rate Variability): How the body adapts to changes in stress and other external factors.
3. **Sleep**: How deeply your body repairs.

When those three variables move in harmony, every other metric from glucose to mood, tends to follow suit. If they diverge, your system is sending an early warning. I call this your Baseline Code. Once you know your baseline, you can make data-driven decisions with confidence and precision. The irony is that we built machines to measure us, but we forgot to measure what matters most. The AI MD™ Method brings that back to center.

Clarity as a Clinical Value

In medicine, clarity is safety and ambiguity is dangerous. Unclear data leads to missed diagnoses. Unclear communication leads to unnecessary procedures and a cascade of care. Unclear self-understanding leads to chronic stress. Clarity isn't a luxury anymore, it's a clinical requirement; and, in the next decade, the people who thrive won't be the ones with the most data. They'll be the ones who can interpret it the fastest.

That's the essence of Artificial Clarity. It's a partnership between human intuition and digital insight. When those two forces combine, your health data stops being a burden and it becomes a blueprint.

The Psychology of Confusion

Every generation has its version of confusion. Our grandparents were confused by calories. Our parents were confused by cholesterol and now, we're confused by data.

We've replaced the uncertainty of symptoms with the uncertainty of statistics. It's a modern kind of suffering, being "almost certain" all the time. Almost certain your sleep score means something. Almost certain your HRV is too low. Almost certain the app is right about your recovery, but never fully sure what to do about it.

That uncertainty creates what I call data-induced anxiety. It's also been called Alert Fatigue. It's when every notification becomes a referendum on your health, and every score becomes a verdict. Similar to a patient who Googles symptoms and convinces themselves they're dying, many of us now wake up every morning already stressed by our interpretation rather than our condition.

It's not our fault. We were promised clarity and what we actually got was complexity.

The Signal and the Static

The problem isn't the technology itself; it's the translation gap between raw data and personal meaning. AI systems can detect patterns, but they can't yet define purpose. They can show correlation, but not consequence and the human mind craves meaning, not just measurement.

The brain processes information through pattern recognition, too. When those patterns are coherent, it feels calm. When they're contradictory, it feels chaotic. That's why so many people feel stressed by health tracking, not because of poor results, but because of mixed signals.

Your sleep app says "great job. "Your recovery score says "take a rest day." Your energy feels fine until you read the numbers, then start questioning yourself. That's the moment when trust transfers from intuition to technology and imbalance begins.

Artificial Clarity is about restoring that balance using data to confirm intuition, not replace it. When technology serves your awareness, not your anxiety, it becomes a form of self-mastery.

The Coherence Principle

Let's get a little scientific for a moment.

There's a concept called physiological coherence. It describes the harmony between your heart, breath, brainwaves, and emotional state. When you're coherent, everything in your system communicates efficiently; it's the scientific and biological definition of alignment.

Heart Rate Variability is one of the best windows into that coherence. When your HRV is stable and responsive, it signals flexibility, recovery, and adaptability. It's basically the holy grail of health. When it's flat, your nervous system is likely overworked and under-recovered signaling a chronic stress state and burnout.

The part most people miss: HRV isn't just a number; it's a language. It tells you how your inner world is handling your outer world. It's the bridge between biology and behavior and once you learn to listen, your body becomes your most accurate biofeedback device.

That's why HRV sits at the center of your BHI, because it's objective, truthful, and how we measure coherence.

How The AI MD™ Framework Was Born

The origin of The AI MD™ was not a moment of inspiration; it came as the byproduct of my own personal frustration.

As a double board certified physician, I had access to the best labs, devices, and analytics. However, even I found myself lost in the avalanche of data. Every platform spoke a different language. Every graph told a different story and I realized: if I was overwhelmed, what chance did my patients have?

I started asking a new kind of question. Instead of "What's the best device?", I asked, "What's the most integrative path?" The answer came through the very discipline I was trained in: informatics. Informatics is the art of turning complexity into clarity. It's about structuring data so that decisions become obvious.

Once I took that clinical lens and applied it to personal health, what emerged was The AI MD™ Method. A structure that helps anyone move from noise to knowledge, and knowledge to action.

It wasn't designed for the early adopters of Silicon Valley or the professional biohackers. It was designed for everyone who's ever looked at their wearable and thought, "Okay, now what?" That question, "Now what?", is the hinge of this entire book. Knowledge without application is nothing more than noise. Clarity without action is still just confusion.

From Overload to Oversight

What's remarkable is that the technology itself isn't the enemy. It's our relationship with it. We've outsourced awareness to algorithms. We've confused tracking for transformation and we've forgotten that feedback is only useful if we understand how to use it.

That's why the AI MD™ Method starts with Assess. It's not about how much data you can collect; it's about which outcomes you actually care about. When you shift from collecting information to defining intention, everything changes. Your devices stop competing for your attention and start cooperating toward your goal. You stop asking, "What does this mean?" and start asking, "What does this help me become?" That's the turning point from Artificial Confusion to Artificial Clarity.

The AI MD™ Promise

AI should make your health feel more human, not more mechanical.

If there's one thing I want you to remember from this first chapter, it's this:

Artificial Clarity isn't about surrendering your instincts to technology. It's about reclaiming your instincts through intelligent interpretation. It's about using data to close the gap between how you feel and what's real. When you close that gap, something profound happens: your confidence returns and you become the best version of you. You start trusting your body again. You stop fearing fluctuations and start understanding them. You begin to see patterns and progress where there used to just be problems.

That's the journey this book is taking you on. From overwhelm to order. From metrics to meaning. From confusion to clarity.

From Data to Destiny

The promise of technology has always been liberation. Get faster results, better information, more control. Somewhere along the way, it stopped feeling liberating. For many, it feels like a new kind of prison. One made of notifications, metrics, and constant self-comparison.

It's no longer enough to be healthy; we feel pressure to prove it. Every sleep score, step count, and readiness rating becomes a public scoreboard of personal worth. We used to ask, "How do you feel?" Now we ask, "What does your data say?"

That's the world The AI MD™ was born into. A culture obsessed with optimization but starving for understanding. The goal of this movement isn't to make people more mechanical. It's to make technology more human and remind us that behind every biometric, there's a being. Beyond every number, there's a nervous system trying to communicate.

Reclaiming Authority Over Your Health

Here's something we rarely admit: most people don't want to be their own doctor. They don't want to interpret dashboards or translate analytics. They want clarity, not complexity. They want to know what to do, when to do it, and why it matters.

That's the doctor's role. To confidently transform data into decisions and, in a sense, that's what The AI MD™ invites you to become: the informed, empowered, intuitive doctor of your own life. Not in a reckless, self-diagnosing way, but in a conscious, cooperative way. Where you partner with technology instead of bowing to it.

Artificial Clarity isn't a slogan; it's a shift in authority. It's about reclaiming the ability to understand your body better than your devices do. When you actually understand what your numbers mean, you don't fear them. You lead them.

The Paradox of Progress

Every technological leap creates both progress and pressure.

It's worth pausing on a truth that will carry through this book:

We have more access to information than any generation before us and at the same time, more stress about it too. We've built systems that measure everything but master nothing. We've taught our machines to learn faster than we do and we've convinced ourselves that more precision equals more peace. At the end of the day though, precision without purpose is paralysis.

That's the paradox of progress: we've upgraded the tools but downgraded the trust. The next phase of this book is about solving that paradox. It's about Optimized Overwhelm. Exactly how we got here, why even the most advanced users are exhausted, and what to do about it. If clarity is the antidote to confusion, then discernment is the medicine for overwhelm.

A Moment of Perspective

Let's step back from the technology for a moment. When I see patients, executives, or parents, I always ask one simple question: "What does success look like for you in terms of health?" Almost no one mentions numbers. They say things like: "I just want to wake up with energy," "I want to think clearly again," or "I want to feel calm, even when life isn't."

That's the true currency of health in our lives. It's not metrics, but meaning; and, ironically, that's what data was meant to help us rediscover in the first place.

The path forward isn't about rejecting technology. It's about redeeming it and realigning it with its original purpose: to illuminate, not intimidate. To clarify, not confuse. To bring us back to ourselves.

That's why the next chapter matters. It will show you the anatomy of overwhelm, how complexity hijacked clarity, and how to reverse-engineer your relationship with information. It's where we'll break down the 350,000 health tech options into a simple framework of decision-making rooted in science, practicality, and personal sovereignty.

The New Definition of Intelligence

Before we turn the page, let me redefine something you've been told your whole life. Intelligence isn't knowing everything. It's knowing what matters. That's what Artificial Clarity is about. It's not teaching machines to think like us, but learning how to think with them. It's the art of selective awareness - focusing on the data that drives real change and releasing the rest.

Real intelligence, whether biological, emotional, or artificial, is measured not by how much it knows, but by how effectively it adapts. Adaptation begins with awareness.

So take a breath. You don't need to memorize the metrics, chase the charts, or decode the dashboards. You just need to understand what your body is trying to say, and what technology is trying to show you. Once you do that, clarity isn't artificial anymore. It's earned.

The more tools we create to simplify life, the more complicated we make living it. Welcome to the paradox of optimization. In the next chapter, we'll uncover how that paradox formed, how an industry built to empower ended up exhausting its users, and how to reclaim control through intelligent curation.

Knowing what to measure is powerful, but knowing what not to measure? That's freedom.

CHAPTER 2

Optimized Overwhelm

Technology That Promised Simplicity Created a New Kind of Stress

We built machines to make life easier. Instead, we made ourselves busier. We created tools to simplify health, but for most people, it's never felt more complicated. For every app that claims to optimize your energy, nutrition, sleep, or focus, the result isn't clarity. It's decision fatigue in disguise.

There's a word for this loop, optimization fatigue. The constant adjusting, tracking, and tweaking gives a false sense of control that exhausts the very systems it's meant to improve. You start your day with good intentions. Then you check recovery, scan HRV, and sync calories. By noon, you've adjusted supplements, canceled your workout, and spent half your energy interpreting your body instead of living in it.

The AI MD™ Principle:
When measurement becomes your morning routine, momentum won't survive your afternoon.

We've turned optimization into an occupation. It's time to reconsider the return on investment.

When "Health" Becomes a Full-Time Job

In medicine, there's a phenomenon we've seen for decades: the mind can create real physical symptoms. Not imagined, but real. We call it somatization. A patient's worry, vigilance, and constant self-monitoring become the fuel for chest tightness, dizziness, gastrointestinal pain, headaches, and symptoms that feel urgent enough to trigger specialist visits, imaging, and obtaining new lab work. After tens of thousands of dollars in tests, everything comes back as "normal" in true somatization clinical scenarios. The person is not faking these symptoms, but the mind has created them without any evidence of a disease process. In the case of being overwhelmed, the process of optimization is now misaligned.

I once treated a diabetic who checked his blood sugar twenty times a day. Such a process is now more possible than ever with continuous glucose monitoring, but this individual was literally sticking his finger with a pinprick needle to obtain blood to capture his glucose constantly throughout his day. He had fibrotic scarring on all of his fingers as a result. His paranoia led him to come to see not just his primary care team, but the endocrinologist as well. Without appointments, he would just show up and wait for any opening or cancellation to complain about how his glucose would fluctuate all day. His expectation? Instant results to match his instant data. His relentless pursuit to chase numbers was the old school version of optimize overwhelm. Today, this is becoming more of a problem for individuals who have constant data tracking (wearables) with expectations of constant adjusting. Every tiny change feels like a crisis. He doubled meds on a whim and skipped them without much thought. His never-ending worrying and self-directed care was solely based on noise he himself was creating.

Imagine the same circumstance but with AI and wearables in the mix! I honestly believe in due time this phenomenon will become its own epidemic.

This is an extreme example, but completely avoidable with the appropriate guidance.

There is a real danger when wearables and apps turn vigilance into obsession. You can literally hurt yourself with over-attention. A person types symptoms into a chat model: left-hand weakness, chest discomfort. The AI warns, "Possible stroke. Go to the ER." That's sometimes correct, but we know context matters. What if the person fell asleep on their hand and had chest soreness from the gym the prior day? Without context, people clog the emergency rooms wasting their time, receive invasive care they do not need, bypass care or even worse, self-medicate. We've always had "Dr. Google." We've now given it a doctorate in over-confidence.

The AI MD™ Principle:
Data without context breeds fear;
context without discipline breeds drift.

The Optimization Industry (and Why It Feeds on Confusion)

Let's zoom out for a moment. In the last decade, wellness became a trillion-dollar sector. Data became its currency. From wearables to influencer-backed supplements, the narrative shifted from healthcare to self-tracking. Every promise sounds the same: "Know yourself better."

But knowledge without interpretation is noise. Most people aren't suffering from a lack of motivation; they're suffering from a lack of meaningful interpretation.

Here's the uncomfortable truth: the optimization industry profits from uncertainty. The more confused you feel, the more products you'll buy. The more metrics you chase, the more dependent you become. Are these companies malicious? No, they are misaligned. They've mastered the art of metrics, not the science of meaning, and meaning lives in context.

You can't view menstrual cycle predictions purely through HRV shifts and logging prompts. HRV can change for many reasons whether it's late bills, family stress, or a twisted ankle. Without context, the inference becomes a conclusion, and the conclusion turns into a behavior you didn't need.

The AI MD™ Principle:
Measure less. Interpret more.

The Psychology of "Almost"

High performers know this feeling: almost. Almost sleeping enough. Almost recovering fully. Almost at peak.

A 93% recovery score? "Great... but why not 96?" An 84? "Terrible. I'm slipping."

We call this the *Almost Syndrome*, a loop that mimics progress while masking imbalance. Each new number creates a micro-hit of dopamine. When the feedback gets inconsistent or unclear, the same loop produces stress, frustration, and eventually burnout. Behavior science calls this variable reward, the slot-machine logic of "maybe this time" that keeps you pulling the lever. We repackaged it for health.

Here's what follows when you live in almost: health dysmorphia. Gym veterans know body dysmorphia that makes you feel like you're never lean enough or never big enough. Wearables are birthing its cousin: number dysmorphia. Never recovered enough. Never calm enough. Never optimized enough. It's an obsession with decimal points.

You can chase 98's forever and miss the point: human health is dynamic, not static. Scores should trend, not hover. Normals change with age like resting heart rate, blood pressure, bone density, and sleep architecture. As you evolve, your thresholds should too.

The AI MD™ Principle:
If perfection is the plan, dysmorphia is the destination.

Case Study: When the Numbers Don't Add Up

A former founder I coached was tracking everything from sleep, strain, macros, steps, and cognitive focus. On paper, his data is pristine. HRV optimal. Sleep efficient. Activity balanced. However, his brain never turns off. He lives in continuous low-grade activation which is like the nervous system equivalent of having 100 browser tabs open.

He received the same assignment I give executives and athletes when numbers become noise: no tracking for seven days. No watch. No ring. No metrics. Just awareness.

By day four, he texted: "I didn't realize how much my devices were running my day instead of informing it."

He rubber-banded back like most people do, but he learned the line between agency and anxiety. Health tech is supposed to create the former, not the latter. When the tool dictates behavior instead of supporting it, you've crossed from optimization to obsession.

The AI MD™ Principle:
If you can't rest without a score, the score owns you.

When Wearables Worsen Worry

A patient once used his Apple Watch ECG feature correctly. It flagged atrial fibrillation (A-fib) which is an abnormal heart rhythm that can develop clots which may lead to strokes. He felt fine, but the watch was verified to be correct with its heart rhythm analysis. The patient was in atrial fibrillation with rapid ventricular rate. We admitted him to the hospital, got his heart rate under control, anticoagulated him, and discharged him home safely. That's technology working at its finest.

A different person showed me his watch and said, "I keep checking my Apple Watch ECG feature to see if I'm in AFib all throughout the day." He reported to me he checks his rhythm at least four or five times a day. No symptoms. No risk factors, just searching for an abnormality. That's not an act of prevention; let's be real, that's neuroticism and it will eventually manufacture symptoms from stress alone.

Same with pulse-ox at home. I caught my own mother using it idly. "Just checking." "Why would you be hypoxic sitting on the couch," I asked? True low oxygen triggers obvious body alarms like shortness of breath, a racing heart, or distress. You don't need to hunt for such things, the symptoms themselves will find you.

Younger users are more digital-natives, raised on feedback and are more dependent on numbers. The watch becomes a referee for reality: "But my watch said…" That dependency heightens cortisol, distorts interoception (your sense of internal state of the body), and ironically degrades the very variability (HRV) you're trying to improve.

Quick hydration check: Want a no-app metric that works? Look at your urine color. Dark color = dehydrated. Clear color = overhydrated. You don't need a dashboard. You need a glance.

The AI MD™ Principle:
Your body is your best wearable.

Information Overload. Biological Underload

Humans were not designed to process thousands of self-metrics in real time. Our nervous systems evolved to notice big changes like danger, safety, hunger, and satisfaction. It was not built to micro-analyze every heartbeat.

Feed the brain too much low-value data and it stops distinguishing what matters. It's like an orchestra before the conductor arrives with every instrument warming up at once. Noise. When the baton lifts and the sections align, the melody returns. Coherence follows curation.

Track 10, 20, 30 metrics every day and you drown out your body's intuitive intelligence system which is its ability to self-regulate. The body experiences your "optimization" as overload. Stay there long enough and recovery drops, attention fragments, energy collapses. It's not because you're unhealthy. It's because your attention is.

The AI MD™ Principle:
Coherence is almost always created by subtraction.

Intent Sets the Instrument

Think about the gym. You don't lift heavy, cut fat, build VO_2, and taper for a triathlon all at once. You choose an intention. Bulk. Cut. Endure. Each intention determines the inputs for your training, nutrition, rest, and progression. Health data works the same way.

If sleep is your current focus, one focus is plenty. It may require changes in several areas like hydration timing before bed (preventing frequent nocturnal waking to urinate), caffeine timing, light exposure, and a wind-down ritual. If weight loss is your focus, you adjust calories, pound the protein, and amplify movement. HRV can be supportive, but it's not your headline.

I'm at a point where my in-gym heart rate isn't the star. I've learned my exertion curve. I know when I can push heavy weights with my own intuitive feeling, but I did not get to this point without learning my own heart rate. Getting to this state took about a year of learning, feel, and correlating it with my tracking data. I still have my fitness tracker on at the gym, but I glance at the numbers for reassurance before I hit the weights hard or to ensure I met my estimated calorie burns for the session. I will set a goal for my gym session, such as a calorie burn of at least 300 (I normally burn between 250-350) in 50 minutes. If I notice I am far off from my goal, then I know to what degree I need to intensify before concluding my sessions. I add two finishers and a carry. Hit it. Closed the app. Done.

That's discernment. The metric serves the intention not the other way around.

The AI MD™ Principle:
Pick one intention. Let data orbit it.

The Cost of Confusion

The more advanced our tools become, the more ancient our problems look. We're anxious, tired, distracted, and perpetually dissatisfied not because we're doing less, but because we're doing too much that doesn't matter.

We've become data-rich and insight-poor. Efficient but not effective. Busy but not better.

This has consequences. Burnout is now formally recognized by the World Health Organization. Anxiety, insomnia, and fatigue are highest in the very populations most invested in "optimization." It's not the data that's hurting us anymore. Now it's the disordered relationship with it.

Here's the hardest truth: if your mind isn't right, your metrics won't save you. You can look super fit, crush every readiness score, and still be unwell. Life needs wiggle room. A weekly "cheat" meal isn't a failure; it's emotional elasticity. You won't reach meaningful outcomes faster by eliminating joy.

The AI MD™ Principle:
Mental margin is medicine.

The Missing Ingredient: Discernment

So what's the antidote? Not more data. Discernment.

Discernment filters signal from noise. It's the cognitive skill we lost in the rush to measure everything. Every great clinician, coach, and leader shares this ability. They don't collect more data, they simply prioritize better. Health is not found in accumulation, it's found in alignment.

As you approach your targets, many numbers become less important. You'll know your exertion without a graph. You'll feel your recovery without a ring. This isn't anti-tech; it's post-dependence.

The AI MD™ Principle:
The goal is not to need fewer tools;
it's to rely on them less.

Intelligent Order

Let's gather the core lessons so far:

- Optimization fatigue is real. It converts intention into exhaustion.
- Somatization amplifies with obsession. You can create real symptoms from noisy loops.
- Industry incentives nudge you to buy and track more. Your defense is context.
- "Almost syndrome" breeds number dysmorphia. Chase directional trends, not perfection.
- Awareness breaks addiction. A 7-day no-tracking reset can recalibrate agency.
- Focus wins. Pick one intention. Let a short, stable metric stack support it.
- Discernment scales. As you align, you'll need fewer metrics to move better.

The AI MD™ Principle:
Simplify the system. Understand the right things deeply.

The Illusion of Precision

In the next chapter, we'll examine why even the most sophisticated data can still mislead you and how the illusion of precision creates blind spots. You'll learn how to tell the difference between progress and performance, because the real question isn't how much you're tracking. It's how much you're actually transforming.

CHAPTER 3

The Metrics Mirage

Why Precision Isn't Always Progress

Numbers give us comfort. They feel concrete, objective, and trustworthy. A sleep score of 92 feels like success. A recovery score of 54 feels like failure. A HRV spike can feel like triumph. The more precise the number, the more authority we assign to it.

When it comes to health, precision can be deceiving. Welcome to the Metrics Mirage.

We live in an era obsessed with what can be measured. Every step, heartbeat, and breath that spikes or drops is captured. This fluctuation is rapidly categorized and converted into a score. Metrics promise mastery, but without context, they often create confusion disguised as certainty.

This chapter exposes why even the most advanced health data can mislead you. How the illusion of precision creates blind spots, and why the real measure of health is transformation, not tracking. In healthcare, the numbers do not always tell the whole story. Understanding this is going to be a key insight you must have in order to achieve the transformation you seek!

The Seduction of Numbers

Humans naturally trust numbers. They're clean. They're binary. They don't argue. They don't fluctuate unless we interpret them as evidence of progress or failure.

The thing is health is not a math problem. It's a living, dynamic system. A lab value that might be benign and normal for one person could be pathologic and disease inferring for another. This is not meant to scare you, rather to warn you to not fall victim to the seduction of numbers.

Take heart rate variability. It's one of the valuable indicators of nervous system resilience. HRV gives us insight into the autonomic nervous system's response to stress. A higher HRV generally reflects adaptability. This means you are better able to regulate physiological and emotional stress responses. A lower HRV generally reflects the body is under strain and less resilience. Despite these statements, be careful not to fall victim to the seduction of numbers as even HRV is shaped by dozens of factors. Here is a small list of what can affect our HRV:

- A stressful conversation
- A flirty conversation
- Dehydration or overhydration
- Food timing
- Sleep position
- Hormonal fluctuations
- Alcohol
- Cannabinoids
- Allergies
- Room temperature
- Emotional conflict or excitement
- Overthinking

One day it dips because you had a late meal. Another day it rises because you unconsciously took three slow breaths before bed. Yet many people interpret these changes as final judgments on their health. There are almost an infinite number of possible causes of "spot" shifts in HRV. A single value in time cannot be telling by itself. Let that sink in for a moment and give yourself mental margin.

Here's the truth every clinician knows: Numbers describe reality. They do not define it. Wearables offer precision, but without context, precision becomes an illusion.

Precision Without Meaning

In medicine, no number is absolute. Every lab has a margin of error or variability of being "normal" depending on the population. Every device has limitations. Every algorithm has a bias. This isn't just a flaw, it's the nature of biology. Yet many people treat their metrics like scripture. They assume precision in measurement equals meaning. Exact equals correct. Truth be told, accuracy is not the same as relevance.

You can have a normal blood panel and still feel exhausted. You can have a perfect sleep score and still wake up anxious. You can have a high HRV and still be emotionally depleted.The problem isn't the data. The problem is assuming data is the whole story. The most sophisticated devices on the market cannot exactly measure:

- Emotional resilience
- Psychological strain
- Loneliness
- Passion
- Purpose
- Grief
- Hope
- Mental load
- Identity stress
- The weight of responsibility

Yet these forces influence health more strongly than any wearable ever will. This is why the Metrics Mirage is so dangerous. It tricks people into chasing numbers instead of understanding themselves.

Progress vs. Performance

One of the biggest mistakes people make is confusing performance metrics with progress metrics. Performance is how you're doing *today.* Progress is how you're changing *over time.* When it comes to health, it is all about the *long* game. Routines lead to improvements which lead to resilience which leads to disease prevention which leads to more productive and active lives. Both health and disease are not overnight events. What you set in motion improves performance, but is measured by progress.

A bad night of sleep is performance. Your 90-day sleep trend is progress. A glucose spike after a night of desserts is performance. Your metabolic flexibility over six months is progress. A low recovery score is performance. Your resilience across a season of life is progress. Wearables make performance feel like progress and that is where overwhelm begins. It is how you stack your gains and losses over time that results in the progress towards your goals.

Clinically, we never evaluate a patient based on a single data point. We look for trends, patterns, and context. One number is a moment. Ten numbers are a pattern. A hundred numbers are a story. Health is a long arc phenomenon. You don't measure it in days, you measure it in seasons. This is why most people generally do not need to see their doctor more than annual check ups. Time with routines needs to pass so that meaningful decisions can be made. Unless you are actively adjusting therapeutics or managing an acute circumstance, frequency of doctor visits is not always helpful.

Why Sophisticated Data Still Misleads

Even the best devices cannot escape three unavoidable truths:

1. Each device measures differently.

Two wearables can give two different recovery scores. Not because one is wrong, but because each uses different algorithms, inputs, and assumptions.

2. Biological signals are messy.

Wrist sensors are affected by temperature, skin moisture, hair, tattoos, vascular tone, movement, compression, and hydration. Even hospital-grade devices produce variable readings under different conditions.

3. The body changes by the hour.

Glucose varies minute-to-minute. HRV varies breath-to-breath. Stress fluctuates second-to-second. Real physiology is a dynamic exchange, not a static measurement. A device offering a single, tidy number isn't giving you a truth. What it's giving you is a snapshot. Snapshots inform you. They do not define you.

The Value of What You Can't Measure

Here's a medical truth every experienced clinician eventually learns: Your body will tell you the truth long before your metrics do.

You can't directly measure:

- The heaviness of a heartbreak
- The pressure of carrying a company
- The fatigue of new parenthood
- The stress of caring for aging parents
- The impact of a fight with your partner
- The edge of burnout

- The weight of financial fear
- The burden of internal expectations

No wearable can detect a broken spirit. No dashboard can diagnose grief. No algorithm can interpret meaning. This isn't poetic jargon. No, it's clinical. Psychological load changes everything from HRV to glucose to sleep architecture. Your physiology does not separate emotional stress from physical stress. It responds the same way.

This is why transformation requires more than tracking. It requires awareness from both an internal and external perspective. Numbers can guide you, but meaning is what changes you.

When Metrics Betray You

There is a dark side to data. It can create false confidence or false concern.

False Confidence Example:

A person has perfect wearable data. Their sleep efficiency is high, recovery high, HRV high, however they're living with crushing internal pressure, emotional exhaustion, and quiet despair.

From the outside: *optimized.* From the inside: *deteriorating.*

We've seen this before even in public figures who seemed physically vibrant but were emotionally overwhelmed. Their data didn't reveal their suffering. Think of athletes who are in phenomenal physical shape, but no one would have guessed they are suffering internally. Performance remains top tier, but internally they are breaking down only to prematurely exit their sport.

False Concern Example:

A person wakes up with a low recovery score. They panic. They cancel their workout. They restrict food. They assume something is wrong.

In reality... They were dehydrated. Or went to bed stressed. Or ate too late. Or have mental overload. Or it was just a natural fluctuation. All of these can lower HRV which will naturally lower your recovery score. The reality of the cause was more of a blip, such as eating late.

The Metrics Mirage convinces people that every change has meaning, even when it doesn't.

Case Study: Mental Load vs. Metrics

A tech founder approached me with immaculate data:

- HRV in the "optimal" tier
- Balanced glucose
- High sleep efficiency
- Strong activity levels

On paper, he was thriving. But he felt overwhelmed, fatigued, and mentally foggy. His issue wasn't physiological. It was cognitive load, a nervous system running too many mental tabs at once.

His body wasn't failing him. His mind was flooding him. Seven days without tracking exposed the truth. He had been outsourcing his internal awareness to his devices. This is common. People use metrics as a substitute for self-reflection, but the body always reveals what the dashboard hides. Your introspection needs time and attention as well. Wearables cannot do that for you. Knowing and learning when to pause and clearly see the metrics have temporarily become a mirage for you can make a large impact on getting back on track. The tech founder learned to trust his body more than the metrics and now points to his metrics for affirmation of direction.

The Hidden Danger of Decimal-Based Living

Modern health tech has created a new psychological condition: Number Dysmorphia.

It is the feeling of never being:

- recovered *enough*
- calm *enough*
- optimized *enough*
- rested *enough*
- active *enough*
- ready *enough*

A 93 feels worse than a 96. An 84 feels catastrophic. A single drop in HRV feels like a health crisis.

But numbers were never designed to validate your worth or diagnose your identity. You are not a decimal. You're a human going through a human experience which was never meant to be one thing. Chasing perfect numbers is like chasing a horizon, ever-present, never reachable.

Why Transformation Outranks Tracking

So what actually matters?

The answer begins here: **Anything meaningful takes time.** Bodies adapt slowly. Nervous systems recalibrate gradually. Behavioral change compounds in seasons, not days. Routines must be built and established.

You can track 50 metrics and still miss the point. You can have every number aligned and still be unwell. You can have inconsistent numbers and still be deeply healthy.

What moves your life forward is not perfect data. It is a consistent transformation.

You don't measure transformation in decimals. You measure it in:

- energy
- clarity
- sleep quality
- emotional resilience
- consistency
- agency
- mental calm
- strength
- confidence
- recovery over time

Numbers support transformation. They don't replace it.

Wiggle Room and the Human Factor

People often ask me about my own fitness and how strict I am. My answer is simple: strict enough to be effective, relaxed enough to be human.

I lift. I casually track my calories. I pay attention to key signals. But I also enjoy a whole pizza when I want to. Not weekly. Not recklessly. But intentionally because joy is a variable that no wearable can measure and every human body benefits from. If you do not give yourself the occasional wiggle room, you risk falling back into old habits with old outcomes. Give yourself permission to enjoy the things you enjoy in moderation. What you will find as your journey gradually moves in the right direction, you stop enjoying old habits and subconsciously minimize them. Furthermore, you become satisfied with less. Whole bag of Skittles vs. handful of Skittles. Instagram is full of athletes discussing their "cheat days". Some are notoriously famous for consuming intense amounts of candy. They are finely tuned athletic machines with impeccable routines, but even the best of us out there have some wiggle room. You are allowed to as well.

True health has elasticity. Rigid perfection eventually cracks.

"Cheat days" or rest days are not failures. They are physiological and psychological pressure valves. They create sustainability.

A health plan without wiggle room is a plan built to collapse.

The Limits of Measurement

Even the most advanced metrics will always remain incomplete because certain truths of the human body simply cannot be captured directly:

- Emotional stress
- Cognitive burden
- Relationship tension
- Identity conflict
- Purpose alignment
- Nervous system load
- Social support
- Meaning

These factors influence everything from cortisol to inflammation to mitochondria. Yet they are invisible to the devices people treat as absolute.

Data isn't bad. Overreliance on it is.

You don't need to eliminate metrics. You need to restore their role as support, not sovereignty.

What Actually Matters: The Transformation Test

Instead of asking: "How much am I tracking?"

Ask: "How much am I transforming?"

Here is the transformation test:

1. **Do you feel more energy?**
   Not just according to your device, but inside your lived experience.
2. **Do you recover faster than you did 30 days ago?**
   Not perfect recovery, but responsive recovery.
3. **Are your habits easier to maintain?**
   Ease is a sign of biological alignment.
4. **Is your stress tolerance improving?**
   That's real progress.
5. **Do you trust your body more?**
   Wearables should not replace intuition, they should sharpen it.
6. **Is your life becoming simpler, not more complicated?**
   Clarity is the real optimization. If the answer is "yes," you are transforming even if the numbers fluctuate. If the answer is no, more tracking won't fix it.

The Clinical Bottom Line

The Metrics Mirage teaches an important truth: You cannot spreadsheet your way into better health.

Devices give you precision, but precision is meaningless without perspective.

The future of personal health will not be defined by who collects the most data, but by who interprets it the best and takes appropriate action.

That interpretation begins with you: your awareness, your behaviors, your goals, and your willingness to separate signal from noise.

Precision Isn't Peace

The promise of technology has always been simplicity. But health has never been simple.

If you rely on numbers alone, you will eventually feel lost inside them. If you learn to balance numbers with awareness, context, and intention, the same metrics become powerful tools for clarity and confidence.

The purpose of tracking is not to perfect your scores. It's to improve your life.

Transformation, not precision, is the real destination.

In the next chapter we will examine how even the most advanced numerical accuracy can trick you into missing the bigger picture and how to rebuild a healthy, intelligent relationship with data.

CHAPTER 4

Solution Stack

The Practical Path From Data to Direction

Now that we've exposed the problem of too much noise, too many metrics, and too many dashboards pretending to be direction, this chapter marks the turning point. This is the moment where overwhelm gives way to organization, and where scattered tracking finally becomes meaningful transformation.

Here's the truth. No one needs *more* health information. What we need is a structure that makes health *understandable*. We don't rise to the level of our data. We rise to the level of our framework.

That framework is The AI MD™ Method:

Assess → Align → Activate

It sounds simple because it's supposed to be. Medicine has always been a sequence, not a scramble. When clinicians get overwhelmed, we return to the basics. We go back to the first principles that identify people's needs and ensure they achieve them in a safe and stable outcome.

You don't jump to treatment before diagnosis. You don't prescribe before understanding the needs of people and what their goals are. You don't declare improvement just because a metric moved.

Modern health tech broke the sequence. This chapter puts it back together.

The Missing Architecture of Modern Health

We live in a world where people can track over 3,000 unique proteomic and genomic biomarkers, but still have no idea why they feel the way they do.

I've seen patients walk into clinical settings with more data in hand than you might see in hospital workups. And yet, when I ask the simplest of questions, "**How do you actually feel?**" They hesitate. This is what happens when information outruns interpretation. These moments where patients lack clarity is why The AI MD™ Method came into existence. There is a need for a human doctor to guide the AI universe we are entering into with structure to live the best lives we can alongside technology that will help get us there.

The AI MD™ Method wasn't created to give people *more* to track. It was created to give people a way to put the pieces back together. You can't build a house by placing bricks at random. You need a foundation, a structure, an order. If your health stack feels confusing, it's not you. It's the absence of architecture. This chapter gives you that architecture.

The Three-Phase Solution

Let's break down the core structure of The AI MD™ Method in greater depth.

1. ASSESS

Define outcomes before you measure inputs.

2. ALIGN

Match your behaviors, environment, and tools to those outcomes.

3. ACTIVATE

Turn aligned insight into daily decisions that actually work.

These three phases are the backbone of clarity. They are also the cure for the modern problem of "doing more but improving less."

Most people go straight to activations like supplements, gym routines, sleep hacks, stress hacks, ice baths, or red lights without ever establishing their north star. That's how you end up with someone tracking everything... and transforming nothing.

Why the Stack Matters: The Human Side of Behavior

Before we get clinical, let's get human. One thing I've learned, both as a physician and as a person, is that we are not machines. Data isn't the whole story and it never will be. You can have perfect numbers and still feel miserable. You can eat clean, train hard, hit your recovery score and still be falling apart inside. I shared this in conversation recently, and I'll share it here because it illustrates the point perfectly.

Remember the performer and dancer, Stephen "Twitch" Boss? He was fit, disciplined, admired, and had access to every tool modern wellness offers. If you had looked at his metrics, they likely would have been immaculate, however metrics are not mental health. Metrics are not a measure of meaning. Metrics can't always reflect what a human being is carrying. This is why the Solution Stack exists. Not to elevate numbers above humanity, but to bring humanity back into the conversation.

Health is not just a tightrope of perfection. It's a relationship with yourself measured, but also felt. Appearances can be deceiving. Just because you are muscularly ripped and have impeccable physical strength, stamina or capability does not mean you are the best version of yourself.

You need room for real life. You need room for joy, for ease, for that occasional dessert that makes you feel twelve again. If you've ever heard me talk about pizza, you know exactly where I stand on this. Sometimes the most clinically appropriate intervention is enjoying a slice (or a whole pie) because health is not just physiology. It's psychology, connection, culture, and mood.

The AI MD™ Method honors that. It balances precision with permission.

The First Phase: ASSESS

Most people jump into health optimization backward. They buy the device, then ask what it means. They start tracking, then try to define the goal.

But data without a destination is just digital noise.

Assessment means starting with:

- What do you want?
- Why does it matter?
- What will actually improve your life?

Not: "What does my wearable think I should care about?"

When you assess correctly, every metric gains context. And when context enters the picture, clarity follows.

This is where we define outcomes, intentions, and goals as the foundation that all future decisions will rest on. Because if the destination isn't clear, the data will not be either.

Let me give some clinical context to the Assess phase so that you understand how doctors reach your diagnosis. This will allow you to leverage some of the same tactics that trained clinicians leverage to ensure you begin your journey with the defined goal. Assessment is the conclusion physicians make after evaluating your subjective complaints (a description of the problem that led to seeking the doctor visit in the first place) along with your objective data (vital signs, lab results, imaging results, heart tracing and any other procedural result). It is only after an assessment is made that we can create a plan of action to tackle that assessed diagnosis. The pathway to improvement and treatment always begins with assessment.

What do you seek?

In the case of leveraging wearables, *what you seek* with the wearable becomes an important first step. Are you trying to improve your fitness? Do you want to monitor your calorie consumption? Are you trying to improve your sleep? Do you want to improve your cardiac fitness? Are you tracking movement? Are you preparing for a competition and enhancing your performance? You do not have to have a simple want; in fact it can be complex, but knowing what it is part of the first phase.

For the clinicians reading this book, you might wonder why assessment means starting with *what do you seek?* Remember, this is from the patient's viewpoint. What is it that they want? Are they uncertain about their pain and want it to get better? Generally speaking the answer to that question is "yes". When you dig in clinically, there is always a want, even if it's just to "check I am okay".

Why does it matter?

The "why" is also an important element of Assessment as this is what will keep you driven. There will be ups and downs with your wearable enhanced journey, but the why will keep you rooted and driven.

The same question comes into play from a clinical perspective. I once had a patient who was literally deathly ill with an abdominal infection that required intravenous antibiotics. The entire team of doctors was against him leaving and we were classifying him as leaving "against medical advice." He was determined however to make it for a family reunion that took years to put together, and his concern was he would never see some of his family members again. It was worth the risk of death for him. From our clinical end, we optimized him the best we could and discussed his options of taking a couple different potent pill variant antibiotics that might give him a chance. To our astonishment, within a day his hydration status and labs significantly improved even though he had barely initiated hospital treatments. His goal to feel well enough to bounce out of the hospital was met, and he understood if he started to feel worse again he would seek medical attention ASAP no matter where he was. We sent him on his way to achieve his personal goals. It is amazing to me how much a *why* can change people and align the energy of their bodies to achieve a desired goal. This is not always directly measurable, so when you feel down always return to your *why*.

What will actually improve your life?

This particular question in Assessment really requires some soul searching. It might seem simple... If I have better cardiac fitness, I have more stamina to run or bike farther. That is the objective measurement you will see, but dig deeper. What will improve? It turns out improved cardiac fitness will enhance multiple aspects of your life. Quality of life, physical health, mental health, and the potential for disease free years. The list of improvements to your life is actually much longer than what I listed, which is why you should think deeply on this question. The answer is not one element or aspect of your life. The journey improves a great many elements that enhance longevity and vitality. Identify exactly what you will improve and start counting the W's as they stack.

The Second Phase: ALIGN

Once you know the outcome, you map your decisions, tools, and behaviors to it. This is where the role of behavior becomes unavoidable. Wearables track what you do, but they don't track *why* you did it.

They don't know:

- You slept poorly because your toddler was up at 3 a.m.
- You skipped the workout because your boss scheduled a 7:30 a.m. meeting.
- You ate differently because you were celebrating something meaningful.

Your behavior is the bridge between biology and life. And behavior is influenced by environment, energy, emotion, relationships, social pressures, and sometimes the need for wiggle room.

From a clinical perspective, there is actual evidence to back up behavior change for fitness adoption that relies on 5 core components. These exercise standards for testing and training were published by the American Heart Association:

- Setting realistic and simple goals
- Self-monitoring of behavior linked to goal attainment
- Receiving feedback about progress
- Self-evaluating progress
- Implementing corrective behaviors to move effectively towards goals.

If this evidence seems aligned with leveraging wearables to monitor your goals, you are absolutely correct! There is further evidence of recommended targets, but this book is not about that and frankly that can cloud your mind with even more things to track. How you set your mind towards achieving goals becomes imperative. You want to create a domino effect in your mind to where it becomes normal and constantly motivating to achieve what you set out to achieve. Once you are in alignment, then the metrics from your devices become spot checks and affirmations of correct alignment.

Two more evidence-based research points I want to highlight:

- Habit forming techniques enhance long term exercise adherence.
- Self-monitoring tools and feedback support behavioral alignment.

These points were published by the *International Journal of Environmental Research and Public Health*. They basically showed that incorporating routine consistency with environmental cues facilitates automatic behavior. Additionally, patients who were under a trial of cardiac rehabilitation who received habit-building interventions had greater physical activity and increased use of routine consistency compared to controls that did not receive the interventions.

Remember that alignment is about being human on purpose. Mapping your decisions, tools, and behaviors will give you the long term outcomes you seek. Alignment is where personalization stops being a buzzword and becomes a strategy. Your data should fit your life, not the other way around.

The Third Phase: ACTIVATE

Finally, activation is where everything becomes real. This is where we move from ideas to implementation, from insight to intervention.

This phase includes:

- Corrective adaptation
- Real-time micro-adjustments
- Sustainable strategy
- Maximized vitality

It's not about intensity. It's about consistency.

It doesn't matter how perfect your plan is if it collapses under the weight of everyday life. And this is where most health technology fails because it assumes you are a robot.

The AI MD™ Method assumes you are a person. A person with a job, a family, emotions, stressors, cravings, obligations, responsibilities, and a life beyond the dashboard.

The brilliance of activation isn't in doing more. It's in doing what matters.

Clinical perspective once again can help give deeper insight into Activation. There are multiple randomized trials and publications that demonstrate real-time feedback from wearable technologies leading to systematic and corrective changes in daily routines. These devices act as continuous error signals and when you see that you are falling short of a target, you adjust subsequent behavior (corrective adaptation). All of these micro adjustments over time will lead to measurable changes that become a sustainable strategy. The new normal will be the adjusted/corrective changes you have made. As a result of this, you will start to notice changes in your diet routines, physical activity, drive, and even objective metabolic measurements. Once you are in the activate phase, everything does in fact become real.

The Goal of the Solution Stack

By the time you move through these three phases, something profound happens: Your health starts to make sense.

Patterns become obvious. Choices become easier. Confidence returns. You stop chasing metrics and start directing them. This is how transformation happens through ordered clarity, not chaotic effort.

The Solution Stack is the compass that keeps you oriented. It's the structure that keeps you sane. It's the method that finally makes modern health technology feel useful instead of overwhelming.

Guessing Ends Here

The Solution Stack marks the end of accidental health and the beginning of intentional wellness.

This is where:

- Data becomes direction
- Tracking becomes transformation
- Behavior becomes aligned
- Health becomes personal again

And this is also the chapter that transitions us into the detailed breakdown of each component in The AI MD™ Method. This is where we turn clarity into capability.

Next, we begin with Feedback Fog as the starting point of Assess, because before anything can change, we must learn how to see clearly again.

Your journey through The AI MD™ Method starts there.

CHAPTER 5

Feedback Fog

Why Tracking Without Intention Creates Confusion Instead of Clarity

The Day the Numbers Started Talking

The strange paradox of modern health is that most people begin with the instrument rather than the intention.

They do not begin with the reason they want to improve their health. They do not begin with a clearly defined outcome or even a question they are trying to answer. Instead, they begin with a device. A ring. A watch. A dashboard. A stream of numbers that promise clarity before clarity has ever been defined.

It almost always begins innocently. A wearable arrives as a gift. A friend enthusiastically describes how their sleep score has improved. A colleague shares screenshots of readiness metrics and recovery graphs as if they are stock market indicators predicting success. Sometimes it starts with an advertisement or a podcast episode that makes tracking feel synonymous with responsibility. You start to believe that serious people measure their health, and serious people track their data.

So you buy the device. You put it on. And without realizing it, you step into what I call Feedback Fog.

At first, it feels empowering. Numbers begin to appear almost immediately. Scores. Graphs. Color-coded alerts. Notifications that congratulate you or quietly warn you. Yet after the initial novelty fades, something unexpected begins to happen. The data accumulates, but clarity does not. The feedback becomes louder, but your understanding becomes muffled.

You begin receiving more information than you can meaningfully interpret. You begin adjusting behaviors without understanding whether those adjustments matter. You begin reacting rather than directing. And if you are honest with yourself, you may even begin feeling more uncertain about your health than you did before you started tracking it.

Feedback Fog is the experience of being surrounded by data while losing sight of direction.

You cannot optimize what you have not defined. Metrics only become meaningful when they are anchored to outcomes. Without outcomes, metrics become distractions disguised as discipline.

Most people assume their wearable will tell them what matters. They assume the technology will guide them toward improvement. They assume the score represents truth. But a score without intention is simply noise with a number attached.

And when noise is delivered with authority, it can easily masquerade as knowledge.

The Hidden Problem No One Notices

The hidden problem rarely announces itself clearly. Instead, it unfolds through predictable patterns.

Someone places a wearable on their wrist or finger without defining what they are trying to improve. Within days, they are staring at dashboards that attempt to communicate through simplified grading systems.

An eighty-four. A ninety-two. A ninety-six.

The interface is intentionally designed to feel familiar. Green suggests success. Yellow suggests caution. Red suggests failure. The simplicity is deliberate because accessibility drives adoption. But accessibility does not equal accuracy.

In clinical medicine, there is no such thing as a sleep score. Wearables cannot actually measure sleep directly. Secondary physiological signals along with pattern recognition of such signals classify sleep states to give you insights. This means scores, including readiness scores, are not followed by your clinicians. Ultimately these scores are algorithmic summaries created to compress multiple biological signals into digestible formats and approximations, not diagnoses. It is important to realize scores are estimates, not conclusions.

The human brain is wired to assign meaning to numbers regardless of context. When you receive a high score, your brain rewards you with reassurance. When you receive a moderate score, your brain negotiates. When you receive a low score, your brain begins searching for explanations and, in many cases, threats.

> Am I underperforming?
> Am I unhealthy?
> Is something wrong with me?

If those low scores continue, most people do not become motivated. They become discouraged. They stop trusting the device. Worse, they stop trusting themselves.

And in that moment, the device has silently shifted from being a tool to being a judge.

The AI MD™ Principle:
If you don't define success, your wearable will define failure.

The Clinical Parallel

There is a reason this disorientation occurs so consistently.

In medicine, a physician does not order advanced imaging simply because the technology exists. In fact, physicians are rightfully taught that unnecessary testing leads to more harm than good for people. The same goes for laboratory testing which is not performed randomly. Each measurement begins with intention.

Even standard baseline panels that are frequently ordered serve as structured screening tools rooted in decades of clinical research. Numbers never speak for themselves. Interpretation always requires context.

A laboratory result that falls within a reference range does not automatically mean health. A result outside the range does not automatically mean disease.

Reference ranges are built around statistical averages derived from general populations, not individual physiology. Genetics, environment, chronic conditions, and ethnic variation all influence what constitutes a normal baseline for a specific person.

This is why physicians spend significant time gathering history. They ask about symptoms, lifestyle changes, medications, family predispositions, environmental exposures, and timeline patterns.

Physicians understand the human body cannot be reduced to isolated measurements. It is a dynamic system influenced by countless interacting variables.

Now consider how most people approach wearable technology.

They begin by collecting data and only later attempt to define the question. The polar opposite of how clinical medicine is practiced!

The test precedes the intention. The measurement precedes the meaning.

And this reversal is the foundation of Feedback Fog.

The Three Layers of Outcomes

One of the most significant reasons the fog persists is that many individuals have never been taught how to define health outcomes. The concept of an outcome feels intuitive, yet when asked directly, most people struggle to articulate what success in health actually looks like for them.

Outcomes exist in layers. Understanding these layers dissolves confusion and restores direction.

First Layer: Functional Outcomes

Functional outcomes are the daily lived experiences that determine quality of life. Energy levels that allow sustained productivity. Mental clarity that supports decision-making. Emotional stability that allows resilience during stress. The ability to sleep in a way that results in feeling restored rather than merely unconscious.

Functional outcomes answer the question most people truly care about:

How is my life actually functioning?

Second Layer: Emotional Outcomes

Emotional outcomes represent the internal relationship a person has with their health journey. Confidence. Calmness. A sense of agency over one's body rather than feeling controlled by it. Emotional outcomes determine whether someone feels empowered or defeated by their health behaviors.

Emotional outcomes answer a quieter but equally important question:

How do I feel inside of my health journey?

Third Layer: Biological Outcomes

Biological outcomes are the measurable signals that devices capture such as heart rate variability trends, sleep architecture patterns, activity levels, and resting heart rate fluctuations to name a few. Laboratory biomarkers also fall into this category.

Biological outcomes answer the question:

What does the data show?

Most wearable technology lives inside this third layer. Human life, however, is experienced primarily inside the first two.

When people begin their health journey by focusing exclusively on biological metrics without clarity around functional and emotional outcomes, they inevitably become reactive.

Tracking extensively without understanding how those metrics translate into lived improvement causes the fog to thicken. This is because the numbers are being interpreted without context.

The AI MD™ Principle:
Your wearable can measure parts of your biology. It cannot measure your life.

When Tracking Becomes Drifting

Wearables can be powerful tools. However, only if you know where you are going.

Otherwise, tracking becomes drifting and a wearable becomes comparable to a compass spinning without a map. Information continues to accumulate, but guidance disappears.

People celebrate improvements in sleep scores while feeling chronically exhausted. They panic over declining HRV during periods of predictable life stress. They increase physical activity metrics while simultaneously ignoring signs of burnout.

Visually perfect dashboards are achieved while internally people start to feel fragmented, anxious, and depleted.

Numbers do not create transformation. Understanding creates transformation. Direction gives understanding its purpose.

The Intention Gap

The absence of clear goals produces a cascade of psychological and behavioral consequences.

Individuals begin misinterpreting normal biological variability as failure. They obsess over micro-level fluctuations that have little clinical significance. They compare themselves to other users whose baselines, genetics, and lifestyles are completely different. They adjust behaviors impulsively based on daily changes rather than long-term patterns.

This creates a cycle that resembles academic testing performed every day of one's life.

Even high-performing individuals cannot sustain emotional stability under constant evaluation. Human physiology naturally fluctuates. Expecting perfect consistency from biological systems is unrealistic and psychologically damaging.

When measurement becomes identity, fluctuation feels like a threat. And when threat perception enters health tracking, anxiety replaces empowerment.

The AI MD™ Principle:
If measurement becomes your identity, fluctuation becomes fear.

The Wearable Should Support Intuition, Not Replace It

Wearable technology should enhance intuition, not replace it.

The human body communicated physiological signals long before digital tracking existed. Wearables simply translate portions of those signals into numerical language.

One morning, during heavy rainfall, I decided to ride my mountain bike. Why not, I thought? Of course, the trail conditions were dramatically different from my usual rides so I figured this would be fun. The ground was saturated which caused the tires to sink into mud. I wore heavier clothing due to weather exposure as well.

Despite riding a familiar path, the physiological demand changed significantly.

During the ride, I glanced at my watch and saw my heart rate reaching levels I typically only experienced during steep climbs. Without context, the number could have suggested declining fitness.

Instead, I recognized that environmental factors were increasing exertion. Rather than think differently about myself, I thought "wow, what a difference the environmental changes can make to my baseline effort."

I adjusted pacing, incorporated additional recovery intervals, and completed the ride successfully. The metric served as a supportive signal rather than a judgment. It reinforced awareness rather than replacing it.

Healthy tracking involves partnership between intuition and data. The number provides feedback. The individual provides interpretation.

The AI MD™ Principle:
A metric without context is a misunderstanding waiting to happen.

The Practitioner's Lens

Clinicians define intent before measurement through a structured reasoning process.

Patients rarely articulate their concerns using clinical terminology, yet every visit contains an implicit outcome. Relief from pain. Restoration of energy. Control of chronic conditions. Reassurance that symptoms do not represent severe disease.

The diagnostic pathway follows a predictable structure. A chief concern initiates evaluation. History provides context. Contributing factors shape hypotheses. Testing strategies are selected purposefully. Corrective plans emerge from interpreted results.

When this sequence is reversed, the "cascade of care" occurs. To recap in context, cascade refers to a chain reaction of unnecessary testing, unnecessary anxiety, and sometimes unnecessary intervention triggered by measurement without intention.

Cascading care is not caused by malicious healthcare practices. It is often initiated through uncontrolled data collection lacking clear questions.

The same phenomenon occurs in personal health tracking when individuals chase metrics without defining purpose.

Treating a Number vs Treating a Person

The difference between treating numbers and treating people lies in interpretation.

Identical numerical values can represent entirely different clinical realities depending on age, genetics, baseline physiology, and environmental exposure. Even such things as your normal resting heart rate varies wildly with age. As an infant, your normal heart rate can be as high as 160 beats per minute.

As an adult, many people will feel faint, lightheaded or even have some degree of chest pain with a heart rate of 160 beats per minute. In fact, some might even pass out.

Treating numbers blindly disregards individuality. Treating individuals contextualizes numbers within lived biology.

When Numbers Improve but Life Gets Worse

There are clinical situations where numerical improvement does not equate to recovery.

Advanced heart disease may allow temporary improvement in functional measurements without reversing irreversible tissue damage. Liver cirrhosis can demonstrate some stabilized laboratory values while scar tissue remains permanent.

These examples highlight a critical principle: Health cannot be reduced to isolated metrics.

When One Outcome Creates Real Change

Clarity of intention often produces rapid behavioral improvement. Not because biology changes overnight, but because direction collapses overwhelm.

Consistency emerges. Behavioral adherence strengthens. Physiological adaptation follows predictably over time.

Direction does not guarantee speed, but it almost always guarantees sustainability.

The AI MD™ Outcome Hierarchy

Three clarity questions dissolve Feedback Fog:

1. What problem are you actually trying to solve?
2. What is the smallest set of metrics required to evaluate that problem?
3. How will you recognize improvement over time?

Outcome-based tracking transforms data from distraction into instrumentation. This is why I am a big fan of biosimulation. You can simulate your own data trends over time to see if your trajectory will lead to desired or undesired outcomes. This insight not only tells you where you will end up, but how small subtle changes in measurable variables (like your heart rate variability) can have massive impacts over time.

BHI and the First Layer of Focus

Baseline Health Indicators establish directional reference points. Without baseline understanding, improvement cannot be recognized. When intention guides interpretation, baseline metrics become actionable rather than overwhelming.

One Rule for Defining Health Goals

If a single rule could govern sustainable health optimization, it would be this:

Focus on one domain at a time and expand gradually.

Long-term health is achieved through layered mastery, not simultaneous perfection.

What Every Wearable Company Should Tell You

No device can fully capture human variability. Metrics must be interpreted within personal context. Technology provides signals, not absolute truth.

When the Fog Finally Lifts

Feedback Fog represents information without direction. It produces the illusion of responsibility while eroding clarity.

The fog dissipates when outcomes are defined. Metrics transform into meaningful signals. Wearables return to their appropriate role as supportive instruments rather than controlling authorities.

Health optimization does not require endless tracking. It requires intentional tracking.

When direction is established, the journey becomes not only manageable, but purposeful.

In the next chapter, we will explore how to distinguish meaningful signals from distracting noise inside the rapidly expanding landscape of health technology.

CHAPTER 6

Signal vs. Noise

How to Choose the Right Technology and Ignore Everything Else

The Illusion of More

Modern health technology has expanded faster than human understanding has adapted to interpret it. Not gradually. Not predictably. Explosively.

Within a single decade, wearable devices evolved from novelty fitness accessories into multi-sensor biological monitors capable of giving insight into sleep patterns, heart rate variability, activity loads, respiratory rates, temperature shifts, apnea, blood pressure, and predictive illness trends. Entire ecosystems of health applications emerged alongside them, each promising deeper insight, smarter analytics, and faster optimization.

The expansion felt revolutionary. It also created a silent problem. More data did not create more clarity. It created more noise.

Patients began walking into medical offices carrying screenshots instead of symptoms. Individuals started comparing readiness scores as if they were comparing credit ratings. People accumulated dashboards, devices, and apps in pursuit of understanding, yet many found themselves increasingly overwhelmed by the very tools designed to simplify their health.

One of the most common questions I receive sounds deceptively simple: *"Which wearable should I buy?"*

My answer might seem complex as you will read through this chapter, but which device to actually buy is not complex.

Most if not all wearables measure the same core thing: heart rate variability. It is through the HRV that other insights can be made. Devices that have a solid track record of being tested and validated with what they measure generally will not steer you wrong. If you want to wear it and forget it, I recommend a ring wearable. Ring wearables also seem to be easiest to obtain the *most* data, which as you will read, does not equal superiority per se. If you are selective with when you wear your wearable such as during exercise or sleep, a more wearable watch can serve you well. It must be noted that the farther from the heart your wearable device is, the less theoretical accuracy. Ironically, most wearables are far from the heart as they are typically worn on the wrist or on a finger. Devices that are closer to the heart such as a chest strap or wearable clothing do provide a more theoretically accurate HRV. Most of us will not wear chest straps though. Furthermore, HRV-measuring clothing or ear buds are not feasible to wear for prolonged periods of time. Wearable clothing is proliferating, but we typically own multiple articles of clothing and do not wear them for prolonged amounts of time. Other types of wearable platforms allow for journaling to give context to your measured data, which, depending on your desired goals, might be useful. Whatever you end up choosing, the principles I discuss in this chapter are more important than the actual device itself.

Selecting a device without defining a desired outcome is equivalent to choosing laboratory tests before identifying a symptom. It may produce numbers, but it rarely produces clarity.

The newest technology is not automatically the most meaningful technology. The most advanced dashboard is not automatically the most useful dashboard. When individuals pursue the newest device believing novelty equals accuracy, they enter what I call signal overload, a state where the volume of incoming data exceeds the brain's ability to extract insight from it.

In healthcare, excess information without interpretation can become more dangerous than ignorance. You do not need *MORE* technology. You need the *RIGHT* technology. To better illustrate this, it is helpful to understand how physicians start their assessments.

The Physician Never Starts With the Tool

There is a reason clinicians do not begin evaluations by selecting tests or instruments.

Medical training is structured around a principle so fundamentally engraved that students are tested on it repeatedly throughout their education: The first step is always gathering history (speak to the patient and gather information).

Before any measurement occurs, physicians ask questions. They investigate symptoms, environmental exposures, behavioral patterns, medical history, and timeline relationships. These details create the narrative context that gives measurements meaning.

Consider a simple example. A child arrives with symptoms suggesting a bacterial throat infection. The clinical presentation appears consistent with a diagnosis requiring antibiotics. Treatment begins accordingly. Days later, new information emerges showing a viral outbreak at the child's school producing identical symptoms accompanied by skin lesions that were initially absent. The diagnosis shifts. The treatment plan changes. The context rewrites the interpretation. This is also why a simple input of symptoms into a large language model or search engine cannot give 100% accuracy.

Without history, both scenarios might appear identical. With history, they become entirely different clinical realities.

Technology does not replace context. It requires context to function correctly.

Consumers often reverse this process. They purchase tools first because tools are accessible. Devices provide instant feedback. Vendors translate complex biological data into simplified scores that appear authoritative. This accessibility gives the illusion of medical insight without requiring medical interpretation.

The device becomes the conversation partner rather than the clinician. However, numbers without context do not produce direction. They produce speculation.

Physicians gather subjective narrative before collecting and pursuing objective data. Both elements are necessary to produce meaningful conclusions. When individuals rely exclusively on objective measurements, interpretation becomes incomplete, and incomplete interpretation frequently leads to incorrect action.

When Measurement Becomes Meaningless

To understand how to separate signal from noise, it is necessary to understand a difficult truth about biological data. Most health data is inherently noisy.

This statement surprises many people because technological measurements appear precise. Numbers appear authoritative. Graphs appear scientific. Yet precision does not guarantee meaning.

Imagine two individuals presenting with elevated white blood cell counts. One individual is fighting an infection requiring immediate treatment. The other recently underwent surgery and is experiencing normal inflammatory mediated recovery. The numerical measurement is identical. The clinical significance is entirely different.

Without context, the measurement is noise.

In medicine, measurements rarely exist in isolation. Every physiological system interacts with multiple others simultaneously. Cardiovascular metrics respond to emotional stress and hormonal fluctuations alter metabolic outputs to name a couple of variables. Sleep disruption influences immune function. Illness modifies heart rate variability. Psychological distress affects nearly every biological marker we attempt to measure.

Health data only becomes signal when it is interlinked with narrative context.

One of my early medical school mentors once challenged me to list forty distinct causes of chest pain. At first, the task felt excessive. Yet as I began listing different causes of chest pain, I started to think in terms of our different body systems: cardiac, pulmonary, gastrointestinal, musculoskeletal, neurological, and psychological. I quickly realized the exercise illustrated a critical clinical lesson that does not take much time to produce.

Symptoms rarely have singular explanations. Biological signals must be interpreted through layered differential reasoning.

The same principle applies to wearable technology. Without contextual integration, even accurate measurements remain clinically ambiguous.

The AI MD™ Principle:
Biological data without context is information. Biological data with context becomes insight.

Defining Signal in the Age of Wearables

Signal represents data that produces meaningful decision-making.

Signal is actionable. It demonstrates repeatable patterns across time rather than isolated fluctuations. It correlates with functional or emotional outcomes that influence quality of life. Most importantly, signal aligns with clearly defined health goals.

Furthermore, signal has clinical validation demonstrating correlation with physiological outcomes. They produce trend-based information rather than single-day evaluations. And they influence decision-making pathways that lead to behavioral or therapeutic adjustments.

When evaluating wearable technology, signal-based metrics typically demonstrate three characteristics: HRV, sleep consistency trends, and sustained activity load monitoring.

These signal-based metrics provide directional guidance rather than isolated snapshots.

Noise, in contrast, often presents as novelty. It appears as single-event measurements lacking longitudinal significance. It may generate psychological stress without improving behavioral clarity. It may exist primarily as marketing differentiation rather than clinical advancement.

Many individuals become fascinated with metrics that appear technologically impressive yet lack actionable relevance to their personal health outcomes. These metrics create informational density without practical utility.

Signal simplifies decisions. Noise complicates them.

The Health Technology Hierarchy

Not all health technology exists at the same level of clinical significance. Understanding this hierarchy prevents over-investment in low-impact measurements.

At the highest level exists direct medical-grade measurement technology. Imaging systems such as MRI, CT scanners, Positron Emission Tomography (PET) scanning, and ultrasound provide structural and functional visualization that cannot be replicated through wearable devices. Laboratory diagnostics provide biochemical analysis requiring direct biological sampling of your blood that also cannot be replicated through a wearable device. Blood pressure cuffs and pulse oximetry represent validated measurement tools used universally across clinical practice. Of note, wearable technology does not directly measure blood pressure, but can provide insights into blood pressure.

The medical-grade measurement tools provide true objective information that directly influences diagnosis and treatment planning.

The second level involves supportive monitoring technologies. Continuous glucose monitors, temperature tracking devices, respiratory tracking platforms, and wearable physiological monitors fall within this category. These devices provide valuable trend analysis when aligned with specific medical or functional goals. However, their utility depends entirely on contextual interpretation as previously discussed.

The third level involves novelty technology. Devices or applications that track metrics without validated longitudinal significance or without clear clinical correlation. These tools may produce interesting data but rarely produce actionable transformation.

The danger is not that novelty technology exists. Innovation frequently begins in experimental spaces. The danger occurs when individuals elevate novelty data to clinical authority without validation.

Technology itself is not the problem you might think it is; disordered reliance is the real problem we face.

The Danger of Overtracking

Modern health culture often promotes the belief that more tracking produces more control. In reality, excessive monitoring frequently produces cognitive overload.

Individuals begin collecting metrics faster than they solve problems. They compare outputs across multiple devices without understanding algorithmic differences. They track simultaneously across dashboards that present conflicting interpretations. They begin feeling inadequate despite performing healthy behaviors.

Eventually, metrics begin dictating lifestyle decisions rather than informing them.

I have seen individuals present with perfectly optimized dashboards who remain emotionally exhausted, socially disconnected, and physically depleted. Their biological indicators appear excellent, yet their quality of life deteriorates.

Overtracking transforms self-awareness into surveillance.

Some individuals attempt to solve this by layering multiple wearable devices simultaneously. Rings, watches, chest straps, sleep sensors, temperature monitors all collecting overlapping datasets. While certain research protocols benefit from multi-device measurement, most individuals simply accumulate redundant information.

Additional devices rarely produce additional clarity. They usually produce additional noise.

The AI MD™ Principle:
Tracking everything does not create mastery. Tracking the right things creates clarity.

When Devices Compete With Each Other

Another subtle consequence of excessive monitoring occurs when individuals compare data across multiple devices.

Different platforms use proprietary algorithms. Variations in sensor placement produce physiological measurement differences. Optical heart rate detection varies based on skin tone, movement artifact, environmental light interference, and peripheral circulation differences.

Two devices measuring identical biological processes can produce different outputs. Without understanding these technological nuances, individuals often assume one device is correct and another is malfunctioning. In reality, both devices may be functioning within their validated tolerances.

The goal of wearable tracking is not perfect precision. The goal is consistent directional awareness.

Devices should be evaluated based on their ability to produce reliable trends over time rather than perfect point accuracy.

Choosing Technology Based on Outcomes

The most reliable method for selecting wearable technology begins with defining the outcome being pursued.

If an individual's primary goal involves sleep optimization, technology capable of tracking sleep timing consistency and recovery patterns becomes valuable. If metabolic regulation is the primary goal, continuous glucose monitoring may provide meaningful insights. If cardiovascular fitness is the target, activity load and heart rate trend monitoring may provide useful guidance.

Technology must be selected based on relevance to the outcome, not based on popularity or novelty.

Outcome-driven technology selection reduces cognitive burden, improves adherence, and enhances interpretation accuracy. Individuals no longer feel obligated to interpret irrelevant metrics because they understand why specific measurements matter and why others can be ignored.

Compliance determines outcomes. Overwhelm reduces compliance. Clarity reduces overwhelm.

The Emotional Cost of Noise

The psychological impact of noise is often underestimated.

When individuals encounter repeated metrics they do not understand, uncertainty increases. When uncertainty increases, anxiety often follows. Over time, anxiety associated with health tracking can produce avoidance behaviors where individuals disengage from monitoring entirely.

In extreme cases, individuals develop what could be described as metric or numbers dysmorphia, a distorted perception of health based on numerical fluctuations rather than lived experience. They may feel unhealthy despite feeling physically well simply because numerical outputs suggest imperfection.

Health technology should reduce fear, not amplify it.

When Less Technology Produces Better Outcomes

One of the most counterintuitive lessons I have learned in clinical practice is that narrowing data collection often improves patient outcomes.

When individuals focus on a limited set of meaningful metrics, they develop a deeper understanding of those measurements. Behavioral adjustments become deliberate rather than reactive. Pattern recognition strengthens. Longitudinal awareness improves.

Reducing measurement complexity increases interpretation depth.

This principle mirrors many aspects of human performance. Elite athletes rarely monitor every physiological variable simultaneously. They monitor specific performance indicators aligned with training objectives. Mastery emerges from focused feedback loops, not maximal data accumulation.

The Discipline of Ignoring Data

Ignoring irrelevant data requires intentional discipline. Humans are naturally drawn toward information, particularly when that information appears authoritative. Yet sustainable optimization requires learning to filter information selectively.

Ignoring metrics does not represent neglect. It represents prioritization.

When individuals develop confidence in outcome-based tracking, they become comfortable allowing non-essential metrics to remain unexamined. This selective attention reduces psychological fatigue and increases behavioral consistency.

In many cases, improvement accelerates not when individuals add more measurements, but when they eliminate unnecessary ones.

The Future of Health Technology Interpretation

As digital health ecosystems continue expanding, the ability to separate signal from noise will become increasingly valuable. Artificial intelligence will and continues to enhance pattern recognition capabilities. Predictive modeling will and continues to improve early detection of physiological changes. Integration across devices will continue advancing.

Yet technology alone will never replace interpretation.

Human physiology remains influenced by environment, emotion, genetics, and lifestyle complexity that cannot be fully captured through sensor arrays. The future of wearable technology will not be determined solely by sensor accuracy but by the sophistication of interpretation frameworks guiding their use.

Outcome-driven tracking, contextual interpretation, and hierarchical prioritization will remain essential regardless of technological advancement.

The Moment Clarity Returns

Signal versus noise is not a technological problem. It is an interpretive problem.

When individuals learn to define outcomes first, technology selection becomes straightforward. Metrics become purposeful. Data transforms into direction. Anxiety reduces because interpretation gains structure.

The difference between overwhelming data and empowering insight is rarely technological sophistication. It is an intentional focus.

When signal is identified, the fog begins to clear.

In the next chapter, we move deeper into the foundation of The AI MD™ Method by establishing how baseline health indicators create personalized reference points for every future decision.

Before health can be optimized, it must be understood and understanding begins with knowing where you stand.

CHAPTER 7

Baseline Code = BHI

Why You Can't Improve What You Don't Understand

The Starting Line Most People Skip

There is a moment that happens in almost every health journey that people rarely recognize.

It is the moment they decide to change.

Sometimes it arrives quietly. A conversation with a friend. A feeling of fatigue that refuses to leave. A lab result that looks slightly off. A wearable notification that suggests recovery is low. Sometimes it arrives loudly. A diagnosis. A scare. A realization that life is moving faster than the body can keep up with.

Regardless of how it begins, the instinct that follows is almost always the same.

People want to improve immediately. They start changing behaviors. They adjust sleep. They adjust diet. They exercise differently. They purchase new supplements. They download apps. They begin tracking. They begin optimizing.

Usually in the urgency to improve, they unknowingly skip the most important step.

They never truly understand where they are starting from.

In medicine, we call this baseline. In The AI MD™ framework, we call it your Baseline Health Indicator, or BHI.

Without it, improvement is guesswork disguised as progress. Without it, effort becomes movement without direction. Without it, health optimization becomes indistinguishable from health anxiety.

You cannot improve something you do not understand and understanding begins with knowing your starting line.

Why Baseline Matters More Than Motivation

Motivation is powerful, but it is unreliable. It rises quickly and can fade just as quickly. Baseline, on the other hand, is grounding. It is factual. It is stabilizing.

In clinical medicine, baseline data shapes every decision we make. Before we prescribe medication, we establish baseline labs and vital signs. Think of your blood pressure. No doctor prescribes blood pressure lowering medication without confirmation of your baseline pressure. Same on the disease front. Before we determine disease progression, we establish baseline symptoms.

Baseline tells us three essential things:

- What is normal for you?
- What is abnormal for you?
- Will changes truly make a meaningful difference for you?

All three of these are important, but most important from a clinical standpoint is whether or not changes will make a meaningful difference. If no meaningful clinical change would be anticipated, often we do not change actions or therapeutics. You might have a benign condition that causes certain lab markers to be "abnormal." Knowing the diagnosis and understanding the benign nature basically means this abnormality is normal for you and there is literally nothing for you to do about it. It will always remain with you and plays no role in your overall longevity. The treatment is doing nothing.

Without a baseline, a single measurement becomes misleading. A heart rate of 55 could be excellent for one person and concerning for another. An HRV value could represent recovery in one individual and chronic stress in another. A sleep pattern might be ideal for someone's genetics while representing disruption for someone else.

The human body does not operate on universal numbers. It operates on relative stability. And stability can only be measured against your own pattern.

This is where most modern tracking systems fail people. They present averages. They present comparisons. They present general population benchmarks. But they do not always help individuals understand their personal biological signature.

Baseline is not about comparison. It is about calibration and knowing where you stand in proximity to you.

The Three Signals That Form Your Baseline Code

In The AI MD™ model, we simplify baseline measurement into three foundational signals. Not because they are the only signals that matter, but because they provide the most consistent, trendable, and clinically relevant insight into overall system performance.

These three signals form your **Baseline Health Indicator**:

- Heart Rate Variability
- Sleep Patterns
- Activity Output

Together, they create a dynamic portrait of how your nervous system, recovery systems, and energy expenditure systems interact with each other.

These three metrics are not random. They represent the core biological rhythms that govern performance, resilience, and longevity.

Heart Rate Variability reflects nervous system adaptability. Sleep reflects restoration and neurological repair. Activity reflects energy demand and metabolic engagement.

If these three systems are stable, the body tends to function predictably. When they destabilize, the earliest signals of dysfunction often begin there.

The power of BHI is not in isolated readings. The power of BHI is in pattern recognition across time.

Heart Rate Variability: The Nervous System Conversation

Heart Rate Variability is often misunderstood because people assume it measures heart strength. It does not. It measures the variability between heartbeats, which reflects the balance between the sympathetic and parasympathetic branches of the autonomic nervous system.

In simple terms, HRV is a conversation between stress and recovery.

Higher variability generally reflects greater adaptability. Lower variability may reflect fatigue, illness, psychological stress, or physiological overload.

But HRV must always be interpreted through your baseline. A value that is low for one individual may be normal for another. HRV is deeply influenced by genetics, age, fitness level, and chronic health patterns as mentioned.

In medicine, context always overrides raw measurement. HRV is no different.

A sudden drop in HRV compared to personal baseline may signal early illness, overtraining, emotional distress, or sleep disruption. A gradual improvement in HRV across months may reflect improved fitness, improved stress resilience, or improved recovery efficiency.

The value of HRV is not its number. The value of HRV is its direction and trend.

Sleep: The Biological Reset System

Sleep is often treated as a lifestyle variable. Clinically, it is one of the most powerful physiological regulators in the human body.

Sleep influences hormone regulation, immune function, metabolic control, neurological repair, memory consolidation, and emotional processing. Few biological processes operate independently of sleep quality.

Modern wearables attempt to categorize sleep into stages: REM, deep sleep, light sleep, total duration. These classifications can be helpful, but they must always be interpreted as approximations, not clinical analyses.

The most valuable insight from sleep tracking is consistency of pattern and perceived functional restoration.

In medicine, we are often less concerned with achieving a perfect sleep score and more concerned with whether sleep supports daytime performance, mood stability, and cognitive clarity.

A patient who sleeps seven hours consistently and wakes refreshed is often healthier than a patient who sleeps nine hours inconsistently and wakes fatigued.

Sleep baseline provides insight into rhythm. And rhythm is often more important than perfection.

Activity: The Demand Side of Human Performance

Activity is the third component of BHI, and it represents the demand placed on the body's energy systems.

Activity tracking often focuses on step counts, calorie expenditure, or exercise intensity. These measurements provide useful information, but their deeper significance lies in how they interact with recovery and nervous system balance.

High activity without adequate recovery produces fatigue. Low activity with adequate recovery produces stagnation. Balanced activity with balanced recovery produces adaptation.

Activity baseline reveals how your body responds to workload. It helps identify the threshold where performance improves versus the threshold where performance deteriorates.

In sports medicine and rehabilitation, activity progression is rarely linear. It is titrated. It is adjusted based on response. BHI provides a mechanism to observe that response in real time.

Why These Three Metrics Work Together

One metric rarely tells the full story of human physiology. The value of BHI emerges when these three signals are interpreted as an integrated system.

If activity increases while HRV remains stable and sleep remains restorative, adaptation is occurring. If activity increases while HRV declines and sleep deteriorates, overload is occurring. If activity decreases while HRV improves and sleep stabilizes, recovery is occurring.

This triangulation allows for early detection of imbalance long before symptoms appear. This is a key point for how you can use wearable data to anticipate your own personal needs before an undesired outcome advances.

In clinical practice, early detection is the most valuable form of medicine. Prevention is rarely dramatic, but it is profoundly effective.

The Danger of Skipping Baseline

When individuals begin modifying behavior without baseline data, they lose the ability to determine whether change is helpful, harmful, or neutral.

They begin chasing outcomes without understanding inputs. They adjust their diet based on external advice. They alter exercise intensity based on trends they do not fully understand. They interpret short-term fluctuations as failure or success without recognizing that biological systems operate in waves, not straight lines.

This creates frustration. It creates inconsistency. And eventually, it creates abandonment of tracking altogether. There is no longer any excuse to begin a change process for your health without having baseline data. For me, this includes even diet changes. Know thyself first, then you will learn which diets really work for you.

By now, it should be clear your health is based on *many* variables. There is never just one baseline factor such as your weight.

Baseline is not exciting. It requires patience. It requires observation before action. But it is the foundation that transforms tracking into strategy.

Personal Variability: The Hidden Complexity of Human Biology

One of the most important realities in medicine is that normal is individualized.

There are individuals whose laboratory values remain slightly outside standard reference ranges for their entire lives without disease. There are individuals whose sleep patterns deviate from general population norms yet produce exceptional performance. There are individuals whose HRV remains consistently lower than average despite excellent health.

The body is influenced by genetics, environment, psychology, lifestyle, and disease history, as mentioned a few times before. Population averages are useful guidelines, but they cannot replace individual baselines. The hidden complexities of human biology indicate that you might not be abnormal even though your numerical values fall outside of "normal."

This is why two individuals wearing identical devices can receive identical scores and experience completely different health realities.

Personal variability is not a flaw in measurement. It is the reality of biology.

Baseline as Predictive Insight

One of the most exciting applications of BHI is predictive health monitoring.

Changes in HRV and sleep patterns often precede symptomatic illness. Declines in activity tolerance often precede metabolic dysfunction. Shifts in recovery patterns often precede burnout or psychological fatigue.

Predictive monitoring does not eliminate disease, but it allows earlier recognition. Earlier recognition allows earlier intervention. Earlier intervention reduces long-term consequences.

In clinical cardiology, early detection of cardiac remodeling (changes in heart size, shape, and function) dramatically improves outcomes with early interventions. In endocrinology, early detection of metabolic shifts can prevent diabetes altogether. In neurology, early detection of sleep disruptions along with corrective action can prevent or prolong pathways to dementia.

Baseline monitoring gives individuals the opportunity to recognize change before a crisis appears.

The Psychological Benefit of Knowing Your Baseline

There is another benefit of baseline that is rarely discussed. Clarity reduces anxiety.

Patients often experience tremendous psychological relief when they understand their baseline health pattern. Uncertainty is one of the most powerful drivers of fear. When individuals do not understand their body, every symptom feels unpredictable. Every fluctuation feels dangerous.

When the baseline is established, fluctuations gain context. Context creates reassurance. Reassurance creates confidence.

This does not mean baseline eliminates health concerns. It means baseline provides a reference point that allows individuals to respond rationally rather than react emotionally.

Why BHI Must Come Before Advanced Metrics

Modern health technology offers an expanding universe of measurements. Continuous glucose monitoring. Hormonal tracking. Temperature variability. Respiratory pattern analytics. Microbiome analysis. Genetic profiling.

These technologies are valuable when used correctly. But without foundational baseline data, advanced metrics often produce more confusion than clarity.

BHI provides system-level insight. Advanced metrics provide subsystem detail. Subsystem detail without system understanding leads to fragmented decision-making.

In medicine, specialists often collaborate because individual organ systems influence each other. Amongst many different factors, cardiologists rely on metabolic data. Endocrinologists rely on neurological patterns. Psychiatrists rely on sleep architecture.

This is overly simplified, but health is never isolated. BHI respects that integration.

Establishing Your Baseline Code

Establishing a baseline requires observation across time. It requires consistency in tracking. It requires resisting the urge to immediately modify behavior.

In most cases, baseline requires several weeks of stable monitoring. Patterns begin to emerge. Variability ranges become visible. Recovery patterns become predictable.

Only after baseline stability is recognized should behavior modification begin.

Baseline is not a passive process. It is an active investigation.

The AI MD™ Principle:
Baseline before breakthrough.

Every optimization journey is built on awareness. Awareness is built on measurement. Measurement is built on baseline.

Without baseline, improvement is invisible. Without baseline, regression is unrecognized. Without baseline, strategy is speculation. Baseline is not the destination. It is the starting point on the map.

Learning to Listen Before You Lead

The modern world encourages immediate action. Faster results. Faster improvements. Faster transformation.

Biology does not operate at digital speed. It operates at biological speed. It requires observation before intervention. It requires listening before leadership.

Your baseline code is the first conversation you have with your body in the language of data.

When you understand your baseline, you stop reacting to isolated numbers. You begin recognizing patterns. You begin predicting changes. You begin collaborating with your physiology rather than fighting it.

In the next chapter, we will move from understanding baseline to understanding how behavior can be intentionally modified based on baseline patterns. We will explore how small, targeted changes can produce disproportionate improvements when they are aligned with your personal biological blueprint.

Once you understand where you are starting, the question is no longer whether you can improve. The question becomes how precisely you can adapt.

CHAPTER 8

Bioadaptive Behavior

Why Personal Modification Plans Must Evolve With You

The Illusion of Static Health

One of the most persistent misconceptions in modern health optimization is the belief that success comes from finding the perfect plan. People spend years searching for the ideal workout routine, the ideal supplement stack, the ideal sleep schedule, or the ideal diet. They treat health like a puzzle with a final solved state, as if once the right combination is discovered, they can simply maintain it forever.

Medicine does not work this way. Human biology does not work this way. Life certainly does not work this way.

Health is dynamic because you are dynamic. Every physiological system inside your body is responding constantly to internal and external influences. Your nervous system responds to stress. Your endocrine system responds to sleep and nutrition. Your immune system responds to environmental exposure. Your cardiovascular system responds to physical demand. Even your metabolism adjusts continuously to energy intake, hormone shifts, and aging.

The plan that worked last year may not work this year. The routine that worked last month may not work next month. Sometimes, the strategy that worked yesterday may not even work tomorrow.

This is just biology alignment.

The problem is that most health plans are written as if biology were static. They assume consistency without accounting for variability. They assume compliance without accounting for adaptation. They assume improvement will occur in a straight line, when in reality, progress in physiology almost always follows a fluctuating pattern.

This is where Bioadaptive Behavior begins. It is the transition from following rigid prescriptions to building responsive strategies. It is the understanding that sustainable health requires flexibility guided by intelligence, not discipline driven by repetition alone.

True optimization is not about finding one perfect plan. It is about developing a system that evolves as you evolve.

Why One-Size Plans Fail Almost Everyone

There is a reason generic health plans dominate the wellness industry. They are simple to distribute. They are easy to market. They create the illusion of structure. Most importantly, they scale easily.

However, scalability and effectiveness are not the same thing.

A generic fitness program assumes the same recovery capacity across different people. A generic nutrition plan assumes the same metabolic response across different bodies. A generic sleep routine assumes identical circadian rhythms across individuals.

These assumptions collapse quickly in real life.

Two people can follow the exact same training routine and experience completely different results. One person may feel energized and progress steadily. The other may experience fatigue, injury, or plateau. Two people can follow the exact same diet and experience opposite metabolic outcomes.

One may improve blood glucose regulation. The other may see minimal change or even worsening markers.

The difference is not discipline. The difference is physiology.

Every individual operates within a unique biological environment shaped by genetics, stress exposure, sleep history, hormonal regulation, inflammatory patterns, and lifestyle demands. When a plan ignores these variables, it becomes fragile. It works temporarily, if at all, and often fails unpredictably.

This is why many high-performing individuals experience cycles of motivation followed by burnout. They commit intensely to a strategy that does not account for their biological response. When their results plateau or regress, they assume the solution is more effort, not a different approach.

In medicine, if a treatment is not producing the expected outcome, we do not simply increase intensity without reassessment. We reassess the diagnosis and the therapeutic responses. We reassess contributing factors or complications. We adjust the intervention based on response. In some cases we even deviate from the norm in terms of therapeutics. Medicine is and always will be custom to you as an individual.

Health optimization requires the same clinical logic.

The Body Is Always Negotiating

Every behavioral change creates a biological negotiation inside the body. When you increase exercise intensity, your cardiovascular system adapts by improving oxygen efficiency. Your muscular system adapts through hypertrophy and neuromuscular coordination. Your endocrine system adapts by altering hormonal signaling.

But adaptation is not unlimited.

If physical demand exceeds recovery capacity, the body begins compensating rather than improving. Sleep disturbances increase. Stress hormones elevate. Immune resilience declines. Performance may initially improve, then plateau, then decline.

This is the same pattern seen in overtraining syndromes, chronic fatigue states, and stress-related metabolic dysfunction. The individual believes they are progressing because they are doing more. In reality, their body is redirecting resources toward survival rather than optimization.

Bioadaptive Behavior recognizes this negotiation. It requires observing how the body responds to interventions and adjusting accordingly. It replaces the mindset of "stay consistent at all costs" with "stay aligned with your physiology."

Consistency is valuable. Blind consistency is dangerous.

Personal Modification Plans: The Missing Layer of Health Strategy

A Personal Modification Plan is not a fixed routine. It is a structured system that evolves through feedback. It integrates biometric data, behavioral patterns, and lived experience into a continuously refined strategy.

At its core, a Personal Modification Plan answers three essential questions:

- What intervention is currently being applied?
- How is the body responding to that intervention?
- What adjustment improves alignment between effort and outcome?

Most individuals answer only the first question. They choose a diet, a training plan, or a supplement regimen and focus on execution. They rarely measure response systematically. They almost never modify the plan based on objective and subjective integration.

In clinical practice, treatment plans are adjusted constantly. Medication dosing changes based on response. Physical therapy protocols evolve based on mobility improvement. Lifestyle recommendations shift as risk factors change. This is precision.

Bioadaptive Behavior extends this clinical model into personal health optimization. It encourages individuals to treat behavioral change as an iterative process rather than a rigid commitment.

Why Behavior Must Adapt Faster Than Biology

Biological adaptation occurs gradually. Behavioral adjustment can occur immediately. This distinction is critical.

If someone begins strength training, muscular adaptation takes weeks. Neural adaptation begins sooner, but structural changes require sustained stimulus. However, behavioral modifications such as adjusting rest intervals, modifying intensity, or improving movement mechanics can occur instantly.

When behavior adapts intelligently, biological adaptation becomes more efficient. When behavior remains rigid despite biological signals, progress slows or reverses.

This is why high-level athletic training programs incorporate continuous performance monitoring. Coaches adjust training load based on recovery metrics, performance trends, and athlete feedback. The training plan is not abandoned when performance fluctuates. It is refined.

Health optimization must follow the same principle. Wearables, laboratory data, and subjective experience provide feedback signals. Bioadaptive Behavior transforms those signals into intelligent behavioral adjustments.

The Three Domains of Bioadaptive Behavior

Bioadaptive Behavior operates across three interconnected domains:

- Physiology
- Psychology
- Environment

Physiological adaptation refers to how the body responds to interventions such as exercise, nutrition, sleep, and stress exposure. Monitoring physiological signals allows for adjustments that maintain progress without triggering compensatory decline.

Psychological adaptation refers to how behavior influences motivation, adherence, and emotional resilience. A strategy that produces optimal biological outcomes but creates psychological burnout is not sustainable. Long-term success requires plans that individuals can maintain without emotional exhaustion.

Environmental adaptation refers to how lifestyle circumstances influence behavior. Travel schedules, occupational demands, family responsibilities, and seasonal changes all affect health routines. Plans that ignore environmental variability fail predictably.

A Personal Modification Plan integrates all three domains. It does not attempt to isolate biology from psychology or the environment. It recognizes that sustainable health emerges from alignment across all systems.

When Data Becomes Actionable

Data alone does not improve health. Data becomes actionable only when it informs behavioral decisions.

For example, a decline in heart rate variability may indicate increased physiological stress. However, without behavioral interpretation, this information remains observational. Bioadaptive Behavior translates that signal into actionable modification. Training intensity may be reduced temporarily. Recovery strategies may be prioritized. Sleep hygiene may be reinforced.

Similarly, improvements in sleep architecture may indicate that current behavioral strategies are effective. Bioadaptive Behavior reinforces these strategies rather than changing them prematurely.

This approach requires patience. Many individuals abandon effective strategies because they chase novelty rather than reinforcing progress. Bioadaptive Behavior balances adaptation with consistency, ensuring that behavioral adjustments support long-term biological trends.

The Role of Continuous Monitoring

Continuous monitoring is not intended to increase control over the body. It is intended to increase awareness of biological patterns. Bioadaptive Behavior uses monitoring as a feedback loop rather than a performance scoreboard.

Daily fluctuations are expected. Trend analysis reveals meaningful patterns. When individuals react emotionally to daily variation, they disrupt adaptation. When they observe trends objectively, they strengthen alignment.

This is why Personal Modification Plans emphasize weekly and monthly pattern evaluation rather than daily reaction. The body responds to sustained behavioral patterns, not isolated events.

The High Performer Plateau

A high-performing executive who committed to an intensive training routine and strict nutritional plan experienced rapid performance gains during the first three months. His wearable metrics showed improved cardiovascular fitness and increased activity levels. However, by month four, his recovery metrics declined, sleep disturbances increased, and he began experiencing persistent fatigue.

Initially, he interpreted these signals as motivation to increase effort. He added additional training sessions and intensified caloric restriction. Within weeks, his performance plateaued and injury risk increased.

When evaluated through a Bioadaptive Behavior model, the issue became clear. His behavioral strategy had exceeded his recovery capacity. His physiology was compensating rather than improving.

The intervention was not to abandon training. It was to modify it. Training intensity was periodized. Recovery days were structured intentionally. Nutritional intake was adjusted to support energy balance.

Within six weeks, performance resumed improving. The difference was not discipline. The difference was adaptive intelligence. For professional athletes, they have whole teams that help with execution of such adaptive intelligence. In the age of wearables and AI you too can gather the insights to conduct adaptive intelligence.

Why Adaptation Requires Emotional Maturity

Bioadaptive Behavior requires individuals to accept variability without interpreting it as failure. This is psychologically challenging. Many people associate consistency with virtue. They equate adjustment with weakness. You will always and forever need adjustment. There is no way to avoid it as you age. How much and for how long you need an adjustment however will be less painful than you think if you remain adaptive.

In reality, adaptation requires greater discipline than rigidity. It requires individuals to listen to biological feedback even when it contradicts personal expectations. It requires abandoning ego-driven performance metrics in favor of long-term sustainability.

Medicine has long recognized this principle. Treatment plans evolve as disease progression changes. Rehabilitation protocols adapt as functional capacity improves. Health optimization must embrace the same flexibility.

Emotional maturity allows individuals to separate identity from outcome. It allows them to see behavioral adjustment as refinement rather than retreat.

The AI MD™ Bioadaptive Framework

Bioadaptive Behavior is operationalized through a structured feedback loop:

Baseline establishes the starting physiological pattern. Intervention introduces behavioral modification. Monitoring evaluates physiological and psychological response. Adjustment refines behavioral strategy. Reassessment confirms alignment with desired outcomes.

This cycle repeats continuously. Each iteration increases personalization and precision. Over time, behavioral strategies become increasingly aligned with individual physiology.

The result is not just improved metrics. It is also improved sustainability.

Why Sustainable Strategy Outperforms Aggressive Optimization

Aggressive optimization produces rapid initial results but often leads to plateau or regression. Sustainable strategies produce slower early progress but create long-term stability. Bioadaptive Behavior prioritizes sustainability because sustainable change compounds over time.

In medicine, chronic disease management focuses on maintaining stable physiological function rather than achieving short-term dramatic improvement. Health optimization requires the same perspective. The goal is not to maximize performance temporarily. The goal is to maintain high-level function across decades.

This requires plans that individuals can maintain across changing life circumstances. Bioadaptive Behavior ensures that health strategies evolve with career demands, aging physiology, and environmental variability.

When Adaptation Becomes Mastery

Over time, individuals who practice Bioadaptive Behavior develop intuitive physiological awareness. They learn to recognize subtle signals before they become measurable trends. They adjust behavior proactively rather than reactively.

Wearable technology accelerates this learning process by providing objective feedback. However, mastery occurs when individuals integrate objective data with subjective awareness. They no longer rely exclusively on metrics alone. They use metrics to confirm biological intuition.

This is the ultimate goal of personalized health optimization. Not dependence on technology, but enhanced self-awareness supported by technology.

The Future of Personalized Health Strategy

As digital health technology evolves, Personal Modification Plans will become increasingly sophisticated. Artificial intelligence will assist in identifying patterns that exceed human observational capacity. Predictive modeling will anticipate physiological decline before symptoms appear.

However, technology will not replace Bioadaptive Behavior. It will amplify it.

Even the most advanced predictive system requires behavioral execution. Health outcomes will always depend on how individuals respond to insight. Technology will provide clarity in this circumstance and behavior will produce transformation.

Health as a Living Strategy

Health is not a destination. It is a living strategy that evolves continuously. Bioadaptive Behavior transforms health optimization from rigid prescription into adaptive intelligence. It teaches individuals to collaborate with their biology rather than dominate it.

The most effective health plans are not the most intense. They are the most responsive. They evolve as physiology evolves. They strengthen as understanding deepens. They create sustainability rather than temporary success.

When behavior adapts intelligently, biology follows predictably. That is the principle behind Personal Modification Plans. That is the foundation of long-term vitality.

In the next chapter, we expand this concept further by exploring Continuous Monitoring and how integrating multiple data streams can create Infinite Insight into your health trajectory.

CHAPTER 9

Infinite Insight

Why Continuous Monitoring Transforms Awareness Into Precision

The Moment Health Becomes Visible

There is a quiet shift that happens when someone begins to observe their health consistently over time. It does not happen the first day they put on a wearable. It does not happen after the first week of tracking sleep or counting steps. It happens gradually, almost imperceptibly, until one day the individual realizes something has changed.

They begin seeing patterns.

They begin anticipating how their body will respond before it responds. They begin recognizing the cause of fatigue before exhaustion sets in. They begin noticing that stress does not arrive suddenly but builds gradually, often revealing itself through physiological signals long before emotional awareness catches up.

That moment is where health awareness transforms into what I call Infinite Insight.

Infinite Insight is not about collecting more data. It is about seeing the story that data tells when observed over time. It is the difference between snapshots and narrative. A snapshot shows you a moment. A narrative reveals direction.

Most people live their lives through physiological snapshots. They notice when they feel sick. They notice when they feel exhausted. They notice when they feel anxious. They react to symptoms after those symptoms become loud enough to interrupt daily function.

Continuous monitoring changes that relationship. It allows individuals to see physiological shifts while they are still subtle. It allows them to identify direction rather than waiting for disruption. In medicine, this concept has always existed. It is the foundation of preventive care. It is why chronic diseases are monitored through longitudinal data rather than isolated laboratory values.

Infinite Insight brings that same longitudinal awareness into everyday life.

Why Health Cannot Be Understood Through Isolated Moments

Human physiology is not static. It fluctuates constantly. Hormonal signaling changes throughout the day. Cardiovascular efficiency shifts depending on activity and recovery. Metabolic regulation responds to nutrition, stress, and sleep patterns. Immune function rises and falls in response to environmental exposure and internal inflammatory signaling.

If we attempted to evaluate health using only isolated measurements, our understanding would be profoundly limited. A single blood pressure reading can be influenced by anxiety, caffeine intake, dehydration, or physical activity. A single blood glucose reading can vary based on timing of meals, stress levels, or sleep deprivation. A single night of poor sleep can occur in an otherwise healthy individual without indicating chronic dysfunction.

Medicine accounts for this variability by emphasizing trends. Diagnoses are rarely based on one measurement. Instead, clinicians observe how values behave over time. We examine patterns, rate of change, and relationship between variables.

Continuous monitoring extends this clinical philosophy beyond the hospital and into everyday life. It allows individuals to observe how their body behaves across weeks, months, and years rather than reacting to isolated fluctuations.

When individuals begin observing trends, anxiety decreases. Fluctuations become expected rather than alarming. Progress becomes measurable in direction rather than perfection.

The Evolution From Tracking to Understanding

Tracking alone does not produce insight. Tracking becomes meaningful when individuals learn to interpret patterns. There is a progression that occurs in most health journeys. I have broken this down into 4 stages:

1. The first stage is curiosity. Individuals begin tracking because they want to understand their health better.
2. The second stage is reaction. Individuals begin responding emotionally to daily fluctuations.
3. The third stage is pattern recognition. Individuals begin noticing recurring relationships between behavior and physiology.
4. The fourth stage is predictive awareness. Individuals begin anticipating how their body will respond based on previous patterns.

Infinite Insight exists in that fourth stage. It is where individuals move from reacting to their physiology toward collaborating with it. Once you are in the fourth stage, anticipating your body's response will create the ultimate insight into action.

For example, someone who monitors sleep patterns over time may notice that evening screen exposure consistently delays sleep onset. They may notice that alcohol consumption reduces deep sleep and increases nighttime awakenings. They may observe that late training sessions elevate nighttime heart rate.

At first, these observations feel anecdotal. Over time, they become predictable. Eventually, individuals begin adjusting behavior proactively because they already understand the physiological outcome.

This is the moment where monitoring becomes mastery. You become your own data scientist.

The Human Advantage Over Technology

There is a common misconception that continuous monitoring places control entirely in the hands of technology. In reality, continuous monitoring enhances human awareness rather than replacing it.

Technology excels at detecting patterns across large datasets. It identifies correlations that may not be immediately obvious. However, technology lacks contextual understanding of lived experience. It cannot fully interpret emotional stress, occupational demands, family responsibilities, or psychological resilience.

Infinite Insight emerges when objective data and subjective awareness merge. The wearable may detect rising resting heart rate and declining recovery metrics. The individual may simultaneously recognize increased workload stress and decreased sleep quality. When these two forms of awareness align, behavioral adjustments become more precise.

The goal of continuous monitoring is not to outsource decision-making. It is to enhance the individual's ability to make informed decisions about their health.

The Hidden Power of Longitudinal Awareness

One of the most remarkable aspects of continuous monitoring is its ability to reveal changes that occur gradually. Many chronic health conditions develop silently. Cardiovascular disease evolves over years. Metabolic dysfunction progresses slowly before symptoms appear. Sleep disorders often develop gradually before individuals recognize their severity.

Longitudinal monitoring allows subtle changes to become visible earlier. A gradual increase in resting heart rate over months may indicate declining cardiovascular fitness or increased physiological stress. A slow reduction in sleep efficiency may signal behavioral patterns disrupting recovery. A progressive decline in heart rate variability may reflect chronic stress exposure or overtraining.

When these trends are recognized early, intervention becomes significantly more effective. Preventive action is almost always more successful than reactive treatment. Why wait to take action when we see such patterns? This is a whole new world order in terms of health. *Prevention > Reaction* can be realized within our own selves.

Infinite Insight does not eliminate disease risk. It improves the timing of awareness. It allows individuals to intervene while biological systems remain adaptable.

This is a magical moment and one of the core reasons I decided to write this book. The technology and data insights are here. Leverage it correctly and you too will reach this moment of clarity for yourself.

Why Patterns Matter More Than Scores

Health technology frequently translates physiological data into simplified scores. As discussed, these scores are designed to be easily digestible. They provide a general assessment of recovery, sleep quality, or readiness for activity. While these summaries can be helpful, they can also obscure important nuances.

Scores compress complex physiological information into single values. Patterns reveal the relationships between multiple variables. Infinite Insight depends on recognizing how variables interact rather than focusing solely on summary grades.

For example, a declining readiness score may appear concerning in isolation. When viewed alongside increased training intensity, reduced sleep duration, and elevated occupational stress, the pattern becomes understandable. The score is no longer alarming. It is explanatory.

Continuous monitoring allows individuals to observe these relationships across time. They begin recognizing how sleep affects recovery, how nutrition affects energy, and how stress influences cardiovascular regulation.

Patterns create understanding. Scores create simplification. Both have value, but patterns provide depth.

The Role of Integration Across Data Streams

Human physiology operates through interconnected systems. Cardiovascular health influences metabolic function. Sleep quality influences immune resilience. Psychological stress influences hormonal regulation. When monitoring focuses on a single variable, interpretation becomes limited.

Continuous monitoring becomes exponentially more valuable when multiple data streams are integrated. Wearable metrics, laboratory data, behavioral journaling, and environmental observations combine to create comprehensive physiological narratives.

For instance, continuous glucose monitoring may reveal blood sugar variability that correlates with sleep deprivation. Activity monitoring may demonstrate how training load influences recovery metrics. Behavioral journaling may reveal how emotional stress influences sleep onset latency.

Infinite Insight emerges from the intersection of these data streams. It transforms fragmented measurements into cohesive understanding.

The Danger of Data Without Reflection

Continuous monitoring increases awareness, but awareness alone does not produce transformation. Without structured reflection, individuals risk becoming overwhelmed by information. Data accumulation without interpretation can recreate the Feedback Fog described earlier.

Reflection converts monitoring into insight. Weekly pattern reviews allow individuals to evaluate behavioral alignment with outcomes. Monthly trend evaluations reveal progress or regression. Periodic reassessment prevents misinterpretation of short-term variability.

Reflection requires intentional pause. It requires stepping back from daily metrics to observe long-term direction. This process mirrors clinical follow-up evaluation, where treatment effectiveness is assessed through trend analysis rather than immediate response.

Infinite Insight depends on balancing monitoring with reflection.

When Monitoring Predicts Illness Before Symptoms

One of the most promising developments in digital health technology is the ability to detect physiological stress responses before clinical symptoms appear. Research has demonstrated that changes in resting heart rate, skin temperature, and Heart Rate Variability can precede viral illness onset by several days.

This predictive capability transforms monitoring from observational to preventive. Individuals may recognize early signs of illness and adjust behavior to support immune function. Reduced training intensity, improved sleep prioritization, and increased hydration may mitigate severity or duration of illness.

While predictive monitoring is not perfect, it represents a fundamental shift in healthcare philosophy. It moves individuals from reactive treatment toward proactive prevention.

Infinite Insight does not guarantee avoidance of illness. It increases preparedness and responsiveness.

Case Study: The Executive Burnout Cycle

A senior executive experienced recurring cycles of high productivity followed by exhaustion. During peak performance phases, he maintained intense work schedules, frequent travel, and minimal sleep. Eventually, he would experience severe fatigue, reduced cognitive clarity, and increased illness frequency.

Through continuous monitoring, a pattern emerged. During high workload periods, his resting heart rate gradually increased, heart rate variability declined, and sleep efficiency decreased. These changes occurred weeks before subjective burnout symptoms appeared.

With this insight, behavioral adjustments were implemented earlier in the cycle. Strategic recovery periods were introduced during rising stress trends. Sleep prioritization increased before exhaustion occurred. Over time, performance stability improved, and burnout episodes diminished.

The transformation did not occur because workload decreased. It occurred because awareness improved. This comes back to the point made earlier:

Prevention > Reaction

Prevention does not have to be applied to clinical disease states only, it is also applicable to prevention of burnout rather than reaction to burnout.

Why Continuous Monitoring Builds Trust in the Body

Many individuals experience anxiety regarding their health because they feel disconnected from their physiology. Symptoms appear unpredictable. Fatigue feels unexplained. Recovery feels inconsistent. This unpredictability creates fear.

Continuous monitoring builds physiological trust. When individuals observe consistent patterns between behavior and response, uncertainty decreases. They begin understanding why they feel the way they feel. They begin recognizing that many physiological responses are logical rather than random.

Trust transforms the emotional relationship with health. Instead of fearing fluctuation, individuals learn to interpret it. Instead of reacting impulsively, they respond intentionally.

Infinite Insight is not just physiological awareness. It is psychological reassurance.

The AI MD™ Continuous Monitoring Model

Continuous monitoring operates through four interconnected stages.

1. Baseline establishes physiological reference.
2. Monitoring collects longitudinal data.
3. Integration combines multiple data streams.
4. Reflection transforms data into behavioral strategy.

This model transforms health tracking into dynamic awareness. It ensures that monitoring supports action rather than replacing it. Each stage reinforces the next, creating continuous feedback between physiology and behavior.

Over time, individuals develop an increasingly personalized understanding of their biological patterns. Monitoring becomes less about collecting information and more about refining strategy.

Why Infinite Insight Is a Lifelong Process

Physiology changes across the lifespan. This is normal. Hormonal patterns evolve. This is normal. Recovery capacity shifts. This is normal. Environmental demands fluctuate. Continuous monitoring supports adaptation across these transitions.

Infinite Insight is not a temporary achievement. It is an evolving awareness that deepens over time. As individuals accumulate longitudinal health data, their predictive understanding improves. They learn how their body responds to aging, stress exposure, and lifestyle modification.

This evolving awareness transforms health from a reactive pursuit into a proactive collaboration.

Seeing the Whole Story

Continuous monitoring reveals what isolated measurements cannot. It reveals direction. It reveals relationship. It reveals the story your physiology tells across time.

Infinite Insight does not come from seeing more numbers. It comes from seeing more meaning within those numbers. It transforms data into understanding, understanding into strategy, and strategy into sustainable transformation.

Health clarity does not appear suddenly. It emerges gradually as patterns become visible. When individuals commit to continuous monitoring with intentional reflection, their physiology becomes less mysterious and more predictable.

In the next chapter, we move from awareness into precision action. We explore Dynamic Calibration and how real-time reassessment allows individuals to refine their health strategies continuously, ensuring that adaptation remains aligned with evolving physiology.

CHAPTER 10

Dynamic Calibration

Why Real-Time Reassessment Is the Missing Link Between Awareness and Transformation

When Awareness Alone Is Not Enough

Awareness changes everything, but awareness alone does not create transformation. There is a moment that happens in nearly every health journey where individuals begin to understand their physiology. They recognize patterns. They anticipate how their body will respond. They notice how sleep influences recovery, how stress influences cardiovascular regulation, and how nutrition influences energy and metabolic balance.

Yet even with this awareness, many people remain stuck.

They know what is happening, but they do not consistently adjust what they are doing. They continue following routines that once worked but no longer match their current physiology. They hold onto training plans that were designed for a different season of life. They follow nutrition strategies that once produced results but now create fatigue. They maintain sleep routines that once supported recovery but now fail to meet increasing demands.

This is where Dynamic Calibration becomes essential.

Dynamic Calibration is the ability to adjust health strategies in real time based on evolving physiological feedback. It is the bridge between awareness and action. It transforms monitoring from passive observation into active course correction.

Human physiology is adaptive. It responds constantly to internal and external stressors. The strategies that support health must be equally adaptive. Static health plans assume that biology remains unchanged. Dynamic Calibration acknowledges that biology is always changing.

The Illusion of Fixed Health Plans

Most people approach health using static frameworks. They create exercise programs with fixed schedules. They follow dietary plans with rigid caloric targets. They adopt sleep routines that remain unchanged regardless of environmental or occupational demands.

Static frameworks create simplicity, but they ignore biological variability. They assume that recovery capacity remains stable. They assume that stress exposure remains consistent. They assume that metabolic efficiency does not fluctuate.

In clinical medicine, fixed treatment plans rarely exist. Medication dosages change based on response. Rehabilitation protocols evolve based on progress. Treatment strategies adjust based on new laboratory findings or imaging results.

Dynamic Calibration brings this clinical flexibility into personal health optimization. It acknowledges that effective health strategies must evolve as physiology evolves.

Why the Body Demands Continuous Adjustment

Every biological system operates through feedback loops. The nervous system regulates heart rate and stress response based on environmental input. The endocrine system adjusts hormonal signaling based on metabolic demands. The immune system modifies inflammatory response based on exposure and recovery status.

When individuals ignore these feedback signals, physiological imbalance accumulates. Overtraining occurs when exercise intensity remains high despite declining recovery metrics. Metabolic dysfunction develops when nutritional intake fails to adapt to activity and stress levels. Sleep disruption worsens when behavioral patterns ignore circadian signaling.

Dynamic Calibration prevents these imbalances by responding to feedback signals as they emerge. It allows individuals to adjust training intensity, recovery prioritization, and behavioral strategies before dysfunction becomes symptomatic.

The body does not fail suddenly. It communicates gradually. Calibration ensures those messages are heard and respected.

The Clinical Philosophy Behind Calibration

In medicine, real-time reassessment is foundational to patient safety and treatment effectiveness. When a patient begins antibiotic therapy, clinicians reassess symptom improvement within defined intervals. When blood pressure medication is initiated, response is evaluated through follow-up monitoring. When surgical intervention occurs, recovery progression is continuously assessed.

Treatment does not end with intervention. It evolves through reassessment.

Dynamic Calibration applies the same philosophy to lifestyle and behavioral health strategies. Exercise programs require reassessment based on recovery capacity. Nutritional protocols require adjustment based on metabolic response. Stress management strategies require modification based on environmental demand.

Health optimization is not achieved through perfect planning. It is achieved through responsive adjustment.

The Role of Real-Time Feedback in Performance and Longevity

Athletic training has long recognized the importance of calibration. Elite athletes rarely follow identical training intensity each day. Training load fluctuates based on recovery metrics, competition schedules, and performance feedback. Coaches adjust programming to maximize adaptation while minimizing injury risk.

This same principle applies to everyday health optimization. Individuals pursuing longevity and sustainable performance benefit from adjusting behavioral intensity based on physiological readiness.

Wearable technology provides real-time feedback that supports these adjustments. Elevated resting heart rate, declining heart rate variability, and reduced sleep efficiency signal increased physiological stress. When these signals are recognized early, individuals can modify training intensity, increase recovery prioritization, and adjust nutritional support. This is a key point and why you should keep track of your trends. Never daily, but if you have adjustments in life that are now translating to trend movements in your wearable data, it requires a hard look at adjusting your routines.

Dynamic Calibration transforms performance optimization from rigid discipline into intelligent responsiveness. Giving specific guidance is always difficult as each of us have different needs for performance optimization and responsiveness. Some general guidelines are outlined by the American College of Sports Medicine and American Medical Society for Sports Medicine:

For *low* recovery status (accumulated fatigue), non-exclusive adjustments include:

- Reduction of training volume and intensity
- Increase in carb intake for intensified training (reduces performance diminishment and overreaching symptoms)
- Optimization of sleep
- Implementing rest periods between high-load sessions

For *high* recovery status (ready for intense activity), non-exclusive adjustments include:

- Planned recovery intervals to promote supercompensation and performance improvements
- Avoiding excessive monotony by adding variety to training
- Maintain appropriate load progression

When Consistency Becomes Rigidity

Consistency is often celebrated as the cornerstone of health success. Consistent exercise, consistent sleep, and consistent nutrition are widely promoted as essential habits. While consistency builds discipline, excessive rigidity creates vulnerability.

Rigid consistency ignores biological variation. It forces individuals to maintain identical behaviors despite fluctuating physiological readiness. Over time, this rigidity can produce burnout, injury, and metabolic fatigue.

Dynamic Calibration preserves consistency while allowing flexibility. It maintains long-term behavioral alignment while adjusting short-term intensity. It ensures that individuals remain committed to their health strategy while respecting their body's current capacity.

This distinction is subtle but powerful. Rigidity demands obedience. Calibration encourages collaboration.

Understanding Physiological Readiness

Physiological readiness represents the body's capacity to handle stress, recover from exertion, and maintain functional performance. Readiness fluctuates daily based on sleep quality, psychological stress, nutritional intake, and environmental exposure.

Continuous monitoring provides objective indicators of readiness. Elevated resting heart rate may indicate incomplete recovery. Reduced heart rate variability may reflect increased sympathetic nervous system activity. Poor sleep architecture may suggest impaired restoration.

Dynamic Calibration uses these indicators to guide behavioral adjustment. On days of reduced readiness, training intensity may decrease. Recovery strategies may increase. Cognitive workload may be redistributed when possible.

On days of elevated readiness, individuals may pursue higher performance intensity with reduced injury risk. Calibration allows individuals to align effort with physiological capacity rather than forcing performance through fatigue.

These tactics are how elite athletes adjust workouts.

The Hidden Risk of Ignoring Feedback

Many individuals view physiological fatigue as a challenge to overcome rather than a signal to interpret. They maintain high training intensity despite declining recovery metrics. They increase workload during periods of elevated stress. They suppress fatigue through stimulants rather than addressing underlying imbalance.

Ignoring feedback does not eliminate physiological stress. It accumulates it. Over time, accumulated stress manifests as injury, burnout, or chronic health dysfunction.

Dynamic Calibration reduces cumulative stress by distributing effort more intelligently. It recognizes that progress is achieved through cycles of stress and recovery rather than continuous exertion.

The most sustainable performance strategies alternate intensity with restoration. Calibration ensures these cycles remain balanced.

Case Study: The Endurance Athlete Plateau

An experienced endurance athlete reported declining race performance despite increasing training volume. His training schedule followed strict weekly mileage targets. He believed increasing intensity would restore competitive advantage.

Continuous monitoring revealed progressive decline in heart rate variability, increased resting heart rate, and reduced sleep efficiency. These changes occurred months before performance decline became noticeable.

Dynamic Calibration introduced variable training intensity based on recovery metrics. High-intensity training occurred during elevated readiness periods. Recovery sessions replaced intense workouts during periods of elevated physiological stress indicators.

Within months, performance stabilized. Injury risk decreased. The athlete regained competitive confidence. Performance improvement occurred not through increased effort but through improved timing of effort. This is a classic example of less being more. Understanding how this plays into your personal goals is key to not being defeated mentally and realizing that everyone goes through these phases. Consider it normal.

Why Behavioral Plans Must Evolve With Life Circumstances

Physiological readiness is influenced by more than physical activity. Occupational demands, emotional stress, travel schedules, and family responsibilities all influence biological regulation. Static health plans rarely account for these variables.

Dynamic Calibration acknowledges that life circumstances influence physiology. During periods of occupational stress, individuals may require increased sleep prioritization and reduced training intensity. During travel, circadian disruption may necessitate modified exercise timing and nutritional strategies.

Calibration ensures that health strategies remain aligned with lived reality. It prevents individuals from abandoning health habits during stressful life phases by allowing adaptive modification rather than rigid adherence.

The AI MD™ Dynamic Calibration Framework

Dynamic Calibration operates through a cyclical model of observation, interpretation, adjustment, and reassessment. Observation collects physiological feedback. Interpretation identifies trends and readiness signals. Adjustment modifies behavioral strategy. Reassessment evaluates response to adjustment.

This cycle repeats continuously, creating evolving optimization. Calibration is not a single decision. It is a continuous dialogue between physiology and behavior.

Over time, individuals become increasingly skilled at recognizing readiness patterns. They learn when to increase intensity and when to prioritize recovery. This skill transforms health optimization into intuitive precision.

When Calibration Prevents Injury and Chronic Disease

Many injuries and chronic health conditions develop from accumulated stress exceeding recovery capacity. Musculoskeletal injuries often result from repetitive overload. Cardiovascular strain develops through chronic sympathetic nervous system activation. This can manifest as functional, structural, and other changes that increase risk of cardiovascular disease. Metabolic dysfunction evolves through sustained nutritional imbalance and sleep deprivation.

Dynamic Calibration reduces cumulative overload by identifying early warning signs. Reduced recovery metrics may signal increased injury risk. Elevated stress indicators may predict cardiovascular strain. Declining sleep quality may indicate metabolic disruption.

Early calibration allows individuals to reduce stress exposure before irreversible damage occurs. Prevention becomes more effective than treatment.

The Psychological Benefits of Responsive Health Strategy

Dynamic Calibration produces psychological resilience in addition to physiological improvement. Individuals who adjust behavior based on readiness experience reduced guilt and frustration during recovery periods. They understand that recovery is not failure but preparation.

This mindset reduces burnout. It transforms rest from avoidance into strategic investment. It encourages sustainable motivation rather than compulsive discipline.

Health optimization becomes collaborative rather than adversarial. Individuals begin working with their body rather than against it.

When Real-Time Data Prevents Overreaction

One of the greatest advantages of continuous monitoring is preventing emotional overreaction to temporary physiological changes. Individuals often interpret fatigue or performance decline as failure. Real-time data reveals whether these changes represent transient stress or long-term regression.

Dynamic Calibration uses data to guide emotional interpretation. A temporary readiness decline during occupational stress becomes expected rather than alarming. A short-term performance plateau becomes a signal for recovery rather than abandonment.

This emotional stabilization preserves consistency. Individuals remain engaged with health strategies despite inevitable fluctuations.

The Transition From Habit to Mastery

Habit formation establishes behavioral consistency. Mastery requires adaptive refinement. Dynamic Calibration represents the transition between these stages.

Individuals begin by establishing foundational health behaviors. Over time, calibration refines those behaviors to match physiological variation. This refinement increases efficiency and sustainability.

Mastery occurs when individuals intuitively adjust behavior before negative outcomes occur. Continuous monitoring accelerates development of this intuitive awareness.

Why Calibration Improves Longevity Outcomes

Longevity is influenced not only by peak performance but by sustained physiological balance. Chronic overload accelerates aging processes. Inflammatory dysregulation, hormonal imbalance, and cardiovascular strain contribute to long-term disease risk.

Dynamic Calibration reduces chronic overload by distributing physiological stress more intelligently. It ensures recovery remains proportional to exertion. It maintains metabolic and cardiovascular stability across decades.

Longevity is not achieved through maximum intensity. It is achieved through sustained balance.

Health as a Living Strategy

Dynamic Calibration redefines health from static achievement into living strategy. It recognizes that optimization is not a destination but an evolving process. The body continuously adapts to environmental and behavioral input. Effective health strategies must adapt alongside it.

Real-time reassessment transforms awareness into transformation. It allows individuals to respond intelligently to physiological feedback. It prevents cumulative stress. It supports sustainable performance and long-term vitality.

In the next chapter, we move into Intelligent Integration. We explore how corrective adaptation transforms calibrated insight into targeted intervention, ensuring that health strategies remain precise, efficient, and aligned with evolving biological needs.

CHAPTER 11

Intelligent Integration

Turning Insight Into Corrective Adaptation

When Awareness Alone Is Not Enough

There is a moment that happens to almost every person who begins tracking their health seriously. It arrives quietly, often without warning. At first, the data feels revolutionary. You discover patterns you never noticed before. You learn how sleep affects your mood. You notice how stress influences recovery. You see your energy reflected in numbers that suddenly feel meaningful.

Awareness expands rapidly in the early stages of monitoring. The excitement of discovery creates motivation. People feel empowered simply by understanding themselves better. For many, that awareness alone produces short-term improvements. They sleep a little earlier. They hydrate more consistently. They begin exercising with intention instead of randomness.

But awareness, by itself, eventually reaches a ceiling.

At some point, people know what they should do, yet they do not consistently do it. They recognize the patterns. They understand the data. They can explain their physiology better than they ever could before, yet their behavior does not reliably change. This is one of the most frustrating and misunderstood phases of transformation.

Awareness reveals the problem. Integration solves it.

Intelligent Integration is the bridge between insight and sustained behavioral adaptation. It transforms knowledge into corrective action. It converts observation into embodiment. Without integration, data becomes intellectual entertainment. With integration, data becomes transformation. As we progress through this chapter, the deliberate sequential Integration protocol will be key to turning insight into corrective adaptation.

The Knowledge-Action Gap

One of the greatest paradoxes in modern healthcare is that information has never been more available, yet chronic disease continues to rise globally. People understand nutrition principles. They recognize the importance of sleep. They know exercise is essential. They have access to more educational content than any generation in history. Yet, despite this, behavior often remains unchanged.

This gap between knowing and doing is not caused by laziness. It is caused by complexity. Human behavior is influenced by emotional states, environmental pressures, cognitive fatigue, social expectations, and subconscious conditioning. Simply providing information rarely produces sustainable change. This is why, as much of an AI advocate as I am for clinical settings, just reading instructions or being verbally told instructions by themselves will never be enough.

Intelligent Integration acknowledges this complexity. It recognizes that insight must be converted into manageable, repeatable, emotionally sustainable behavioral shifts. It focuses not on overwhelming transformation but on precise corrective adaptation.

Why Most Health Advice Fails

Traditional health recommendations often fail because they are delivered as static instructions rather than adaptive strategies. This strategy of static instructions actually works well for established disease management or acute hospital pathways to treat high risk clinical circumstances. However, generic advice assumes uniform physiology and identical life circumstances. Even with a static instruction, therapeutics can vary and doses of medications vary as well. Generic advice ignores variability in stress exposure, metabolic responsiveness, sleep architecture, and psychological resilience.

When individuals attempt to follow rigid protocols that do not match their biology or lifestyle, failure becomes predictable. They begin with motivation. They encounter friction. They interpret friction as personal weakness rather than protocol misalignment.

Intelligent Integration shifts responsibility from willpower to calibration. It teaches individuals to modify strategies based on physiological feedback. Instead of forcing compliance with predetermined rules, it encourages flexible adaptation based on measurable response.

This approach transforms health optimization from obedience to experimentation guided by objective insight.

Corrective Adaptation: The Core Mechanism of Integration

Corrective adaptation is the process of adjusting behavior in response to physiological feedback. It is the functional expression of integration. Continuous monitoring identifies patterns. Assessment clarifies meaning. Alignment establishes direction. Activation initiates behavioral change. Integration ensures that change becomes sustainable.

Corrective adaptation operates through small, precise adjustments rather than dramatic overhauls. Large-scale changes often generate emotional resistance and physiological instability. Smaller modifications are easier to sustain and easier to evaluate.

For example, a person who notices declining recovery metrics might adjust sleep timing by thirty minutes rather than attempting a complete lifestyle overhaul. A subtle shift in pre-sleep routine may produce measurable improvement without overwhelming compliance demands.

These micro-adjustments accumulate over time, producing macro-transformation. You are in it for the long game. Being off kilter temporarily is not going to set you back as much as you might think, even in a disease management circumstance.

The Role of Behavioral Precision

Many individuals attempt to improve health by implementing multiple interventions simultaneously. They change diet, increase exercise intensity, introduce supplements, and alter sleep routines all at once. While this approach feels productive, it creates diagnostic confusion. When improvement or deterioration occurs, it becomes impossible to identify which intervention produced the outcome.

Intelligent Integration prioritizes behavioral precision. It encourages introducing modifications sequentially. Each adjustment is monitored long enough to evaluate its effectiveness. This method mirrors clinical medicine, where physicians rarely prescribe multiple new treatments simultaneously without monitoring individual responses.

Behavioral precision allows individuals to build personalized optimization strategies based on evidence rather than assumption.

Emotional Sustainability and Habit Formation

Behavioral adaptation fails most frequently when emotional sustainability is ignored. Health strategies that generate excessive psychological burden rarely persist. Diets that eliminate all preferred foods collapse under social pressure. Exercise routines that demand unrealistic time commitments disintegrate during occupational stress. Sleep protocols that conflict with family dynamics become unsustainable.

Intelligent Integration incorporates emotional compatibility into behavioral design. It prioritizes interventions that individuals can realistically maintain. Sustainable change is rarely built through extreme discipline. It is built through alignment between physiological benefit and lifestyle feasibility.

Habit formation relies on repetition within emotionally acceptable boundaries. Continuous monitoring reinforces habits by providing objective confirmation of progress. When individuals see measurable improvement, adherence becomes intrinsically motivated rather than externally forced.

The Feedback Loop of Integration

Integration operates through a continuous feedback loop. Physiological monitoring generates data. Assessment interprets the data. Behavioral adaptation modifies inputs. New monitoring evaluates outcomes. The loop repeats indefinitely.

This process resembles biological homeostasis. The body constantly recalibrates internal systems to maintain equilibrium. Intelligent Integration extends this natural principle into conscious behavior. It creates a partnership between biological intelligence and conscious decision-making.

The feedback loop also prevents stagnation. As physiology evolves, interventions evolve. What improves recovery today may require adjustment tomorrow. Continuous monitoring ensures that optimization remains dynamic rather than static.

Case Study: Nutritional Integration and Metabolic Stability

A middle-aged patient presented with fluctuating energy levels and difficulty maintaining stable body composition despite consistent exercise. Continuous glucose monitoring revealed frequent postprandial spikes following high-carbohydrate meals consumed late in the evening.

Instead of eliminating carbohydrates entirely, Intelligent Integration introduced meal timing adjustments. The patient shifted carbohydrate consumption earlier in the day when insulin sensitivity was higher. Evening meals emphasized protein and fiber to stabilize overnight glucose patterns.

Within weeks, glucose variability decreased. Sleep quality improved. Morning energy stabilized. The patient maintained dietary satisfaction while improving metabolic outcomes.

The intervention succeeded because it integrated physiological feedback with realistic lifestyle modification rather than imposing rigid dietary restriction.

The Danger of Over-Correction

While integration emphasizes adaptation, excessive correction can create instability. Some individuals react aggressively to minor fluctuations in physiological data. They modify behavior daily, chasing perfection rather than pursuing stability.

Over-correction produces volatility. The body thrives on rhythmic consistency. Frequent drastic changes disrupt circadian alignment, hormonal balance, and neurological stability. Intelligent Integration encourages measured responsiveness rather than impulsive adjustment.

Trend analysis remains essential. Single-day anomalies rarely justify major behavioral modification. Patterns sustained across multiple cycles provide more reliable indicators for intervention.

Technology as an Integration Partner

Digital health technology serves as a catalyst for integration when used correctly. Wearables, metabolic monitors, and recovery trackers provide objective insight that were previously unavailable outside clinical environments. These tools allow individuals to observe physiological consequences of daily behavior in real time.

However, technology cannot perform integration independently. Devices generate data but do not implement behavioral change. Intelligent Integration requires human interpretation, emotional intelligence, and environmental awareness.

The most effective use of technology occurs when it functions as a mirror rather than a commander. It reflects physiological reality while individuals maintain agency over behavioral decisions.

The Psychological Shift From Compliance to Collaboration

Traditional health models often position patients as passive recipients of instruction. Compliance becomes the primary measure of success. Intelligent Integration transforms this relationship. Individuals become active collaborators in their health optimization.

Collaboration encourages curiosity rather than obedience. It promotes experimentation guided by feedback. Individuals begin viewing physiological signals as communication rather than judgment. This psychological shift increases engagement and reduces any shame associated with perceived failure.

When individuals collaborate with their biology, behavior becomes adaptive rather than resistant.

Integration and Identity Transformation

Sustainable health optimization eventually transcends behavior and influences identity. Individuals who consistently integrate physiological feedback begin to view themselves differently. They shift from reactive participants in their health to proactive architects of their biology. Once again, *Prevention > Reaction*.

Identity transformation reinforces behavior. When individuals perceive themselves as disciplined, adaptive, and self-aware, behavioral consistency strengthens. Continuous monitoring provides objective evidence supporting this identity evolution.

Intelligent Integration therefore influences not only physical outcomes but psychological resilience and self-efficacy.

The AI MD™ Integration Protocol

The AI MD™ framework structures integration through a deliberate sequence:

- **Assessment** identifies physiological patterns and establishes baseline understanding.
- **Alignment** defines direction by linking outcomes to behavioral strategy.
- **Activation** initiates targeted behavioral change.
- **Integration** ensures sustainability through corrective adaptation and continuous monitoring.

Each phase builds upon the previous one. Skipping integration creates temporary improvement followed by regression. Sustained transformation requires completing the entire cycle.

The Role of Professional Guidance in Complex Integration

While self-directed integration can produce significant improvement, complex physiological conditions often require professional support. Clinicians trained in functional interpretation of biometric data can identify nuanced interactions between metabolic, neurological, and hormonal systems.

Professional guidance becomes particularly valuable when multiple variables interact simultaneously. Advanced integration may involve medication management, therapeutic intervention, or specialized diagnostic evaluation. Collaboration between patient awareness and clinical expertise produces optimal outcomes in complex cases.

When Integration Creates Effortless Behavior

The ultimate goal of Intelligent Integration is not perpetual effort. It is effortless alignment. When behavioral adaptation becomes integrated into identity and environment, optimization occurs automatically. Sleep routines become habitual rather than forced. Nutritional decisions become intuitive rather than calculated. Exercise becomes intrinsic rather than obligatory.

Effortless behavior represents the highest form of integration. It indicates that corrective adaptation has been fully embodied.

The AI MD™ Principle:
Insight creates possibility.
Integration creates reality.

Data alone cannot transform physiology. Awareness alone cannot change behavior. Intelligent Integration converts knowledge into lived experience. It transforms observation into action and action into identity.

When individuals commit to integration, health optimization becomes a dynamic partnership between consciousness and biology. This partnership produces sustainable vitality rather than temporary improvement.

The Moment Behavior Becomes Biology

There is a moment when corrective adaptation stops feeling like work and begins feeling like self-expression. That moment represents true integration. Behavior no longer requires constant monitoring. It reflects internalized understanding.

Continuous monitoring remains valuable, but its role evolves. It becomes confirmation rather than instruction. Individuals trust their physiological intuition because they have repeatedly validated it through objective data.

This is the purpose of Intelligent Integration. Not perfection. Not rigid discipline. Transformation that feels natural, sustainable, and deeply aligned with human biology.

In the next chapter, we will explore how sustained integration produces long-term vitality and performance through strategies designed to make optimization feel effortless rather than exhausting.

CHAPTER 12

Effortless Effectiveness

Designing Health That Sustains Itself

When Optimization Stops Feeling Like Work

There is a phase in every health transformation that very few people talk about. It happens quietly. It rarely gets celebrated on social media. It does not produce dramatic before-and-after photos. It does not create viral stories about thirty-day challenges or extreme resets.

It is the moment when taking care of yourself stops feeling like effort.

Early in most health journeys, change feels heavy. You have to remind yourself to drink water. You have to force yourself to go to the gym. You have to monitor your sleep like it is a fragile contract that could collapse at any moment. The entire process feels intentional, structured, and sometimes exhausting.

Then something shifts.

You stop negotiating with yourself about whether you should move your body. You stop calculating every nutritional decision. You stop obsessing over whether one bad night of sleep ruined your progress. You begin operating inside rhythms that feel natural instead of forced.

That shift is what I call Effortless Effectiveness. It is a type of automaticity that you develop and is a sign of extraordinary accomplishment!

It is not about eliminating effort entirely. It is about reaching a level of alignment where your habits support your physiology automatically, and your physiology supports your habits in return. You do not negotiate with yourself and your decisions are routine and automatic without much thought.

Effortless Effectiveness is not a shortcut. It is the long-term reward for consistent integration.

Why Sustainability Is the True Marker of Health

Many people define success in health by intensity. They believe that the harder the protocol, the more powerful the result. They assume extreme diets, punishing workouts, and rigid sleep rules represent commitment and discipline.

Intensity can produce short-term results. It rarely produces sustainability.

Human biology does not thrive under constant extremes. The nervous system is designed to oscillate between effort and recovery. Hormonal systems require rhythmic stability. Cognitive performance depends on consistent energy availability. When health strategies demand perpetual maximal effort, the body eventually pushes back through fatigue, injury, burnout, or emotional resistance.

Sustainability, not intensity, predicts long-term vitality.

Effortless Effectiveness emerges when health behaviors integrate so deeply into daily life that they require minimal cognitive and emotional negotiation. The body begins cooperating with the routine rather than resisting it.

The Illusion of Discipline

Modern culture glorifies discipline as the ultimate solution to behavioral change. Discipline is valuable. It can initiate transformation. It can bridge the gap between intention and action during early stages of habit formation.

But discipline has limitations.

Discipline requires constant energy expenditure. It depends heavily on motivation and emotional resilience. When stress increases or life becomes unpredictable, discipline weakens. Many individuals interpret this as personal failure when, in reality, they attempted to build long-term health on a temporary fuel source.

Effortless Effectiveness shifts the foundation from discipline to design.

Design removes unnecessary resistance from behavior. It modifies environment, routine, and habit sequencing so that optimal choices require less effort than unhealthy alternatives. When health is designed into lifestyle infrastructure, discipline becomes a reinforcement tool rather than the primary driver.

Biological Momentum and Habit Automation

The human brain is wired for efficiency. Repeated behaviors become automated through neurological patterning. Neural pathways strengthen with repetition, reducing cognitive load required for execution. This process, known as habit automation, allows complex behaviors to occur with minimal conscious effort.

Effortless Effectiveness leverages this neurological efficiency.

When individuals consistently align sleep timing, nutritional patterns, and movement routines with physiological rhythms, the body begins anticipating those behaviors. Hormonal signals prepare digestion before meals occur. Circadian mechanisms initiate melatonin release before scheduled sleep. Metabolic pathways optimize energy utilization based on predictable activity patterns.

This biological momentum transforms health maintenance from active decision-making into automatic regulation.

The Energy Economy of the Human Body

The body functions as an energy management system. Every decision, every movement, every cognitive process consumes biological energy. When health strategies require excessive decision-making, they drain the same energy reserves needed to sustain them.

Effortless Effectiveness conserves cognitive energy by reducing unnecessary decisions. Structured routines eliminate daily negotiation about fundamental behaviors. When individuals eat similar nutrient-dense breakfasts, maintain consistent sleep windows, and schedule exercise at predictable times, decision fatigue decreases dramatically.

Reduced decision fatigue strengthens adherence. Strengthened adherence reinforces physiological stability. Physiological stability increases energy availability, which further supports adherence. The system becomes self-reinforcing and automatic.

The Role of Circadian Alignment

One of the most powerful drivers of Effortless Effectiveness is circadian synchronization. The human body operates through internal biological clocks regulating hormone secretion, metabolic efficiency, immune function, and neurological performance.

When lifestyle patterns align with circadian biology, physiological processes operate with less resistance. Digestion becomes more efficient when meals occur during daylight hours. Recovery accelerates when sleep coincides with natural melatonin cycles. Cognitive clarity improves when waking occurs consistently within similar time windows.

Circadian disruption forces the body to operate against its internal programming. Effort increases. Efficiency decreases. Long-term sustainability becomes difficult.

Effortless Effectiveness often begins with restoring circadian stability.

Environmental Architecture and Behavioral Success

Behavior rarely exists in isolation. It is influenced continuously by your environment. Food availability shapes nutritional decisions. Lighting influences sleep onset. Social circles reinforce or undermine lifestyle choices. Occupational demands alter recovery capacity.

Effortless Effectiveness requires designing environments that support desired behavior automatically. Removing processed foods from home environments reduces reliance on willpower. Establishing wind-down lighting routines signals neurological transition toward sleep. Scheduling exercise sessions within calendar infrastructure prevents last-minute cancellations.

Environmental architecture reduces behavioral friction. Reduced friction enhances consistency. Consistency creates physiological reinforcement.

Case Study: Executive Performance and Habit Sustainability

A corporate executive sought to improve cognitive performance and reduce chronic fatigue. Initial attempts focused on aggressive dietary restrictions and high-intensity exercise schedules. Short-term productivity increased but quickly collapsed under occupational travel demands.

Effortless Effectiveness shifted the strategy toward sustainable design. Travel routines incorporated portable nutrition protocols rather than restrictive diets. Exercise transitioned to shorter, high-quality sessions adaptable to hotel environments. Sleep routines emphasized circadian consistency rather than total sleep duration perfection.

Within months, energy stability improved significantly. Productivity increased without reliance on extreme discipline. The executive maintained performance despite variable travel schedules because health behaviors became adaptable and automated rather than rigid and fragile.

This case study is so common as many high performers are on the go. The typical approach is a defeated one that signifies impossible odds only because the individual is frequently traveling. The mind is set to accept a lack of optimized health because the being is on the go. Even challenging circumstances like being outside of your normal environment can be managed with Effortless Effectiveness. Once you get your routines and protocols to adapt to your constant environmental changes, the cognitive burden lowers and you can fall into the automation described in this case. Travel and hotel gyms can work for you if you integrate Effortless Effectiveness.

The Psychology of Effortless Compliance

Human behavior resists coercion but responds positively to alignment. When individuals feel forced into health routines, psychological resistance accumulates. Compliance becomes temporary. Effortless Effectiveness reduces resistance by aligning behaviors with personal identity and intrinsic motivation.

When individuals experience measurable benefits from sustainable routines, motivation shifts internally. They no longer perform behaviors to achieve external validation. They perform them because deviation feels uncomfortable. Health behaviors become expressions of self-identity rather than obligations.

Identity-driven behavior sustains itself more effectively than compliance-driven behavior.

The AI MD™ Sustainability Algorithm

Effortless Effectiveness is operationalized within The AI MD™ framework through three reinforcing components:

1. **Rhythmic Consistency**: establishing predictable biological patterns that reduce physiological resistance.
2. **Behavioral Simplicity**: minimizing unnecessary complexity and decision fatigue.
3. **Adaptive Monitoring**: maintaining continuous feedback without obsessive micromanagement.

Together, these elements create a self-regulating optimization system. Individuals maintain awareness while reducing cognitive and emotional burden.

The Danger of Optimization Obsession

One of the greatest threats to Effortless Effectiveness is optimization obsession. Some individuals become hyper-focused on achieving perfect metrics. They analyze every fluctuation in sleep score, HRV, or metabolic variability. They adjust behavior continuously in pursuit of numerical perfection.

Optimization obsession produces anxiety-driven behavior. It disrupts natural rhythms. It transforms health into performance pressure rather than vitality enhancement.

Effortless Effectiveness accepts biological variability. It prioritizes trend stability over daily perfection. It acknowledges that occasional deviation is not failure. It is part of physiological reality.

Long-term vitality emerges through stability, not perfection.

The Recovery-Performance Reciprocity

Performance and recovery exist in a reciprocal relationship. Increased performance demands increased recovery capacity. Effortless Effectiveness balances this relationship automatically by embedding recovery behaviors into routine structure.

Sleep hygiene becomes non-negotiable. Nutritional timing supports metabolic replenishment. Stress management becomes proactive rather than reactive. Recovery ceases to be an afterthought and becomes integrated into performance design.

This reciprocity prevents burnout. It sustains high-level performance across decades rather than months.

Technology's Role in Sustained Effectiveness

Digital monitoring devices provide essential feedback supporting Effortless Effectiveness. Wearables detect subtle physiological drift before symptomatic decline occurs. Continuous glucose monitors reveal nutritional impact patterns. Recovery trackers identify early signs of overtraining or stress overload.

When used appropriately, technology confirms sustainability rather than dictating behavior. It reinforces awareness while preserving autonomy. The goal is not constant monitoring but intelligent validation of integrated habits.

The Transition From Structured Practice to Lifestyle Identity

Every sustainable health transformation progresses through three phases:

1. **Structured Practice**: introduces deliberate behavior change requiring active attention.
2. **Habit Consolidation**: reinforces repetition until behaviors become automated.
3. **Lifestyle Identity**: integrates behaviors into self-perception and daily rhythm.

Effortless Effectiveness represents completion of the third phase. Individuals no longer think of themselves as people "trying to be healthy." They simply live in alignment with physiological principles.

The AI MD™ Principle:
Sustainability is superior to intensity.

Extreme interventions can initiate change. Sustainable design maintains it. The most effective health strategy is not the one producing the fastest improvement. It is the one capable of persisting indefinitely.

Effortless Effectiveness emerges when health behaviors require less resistance than unhealthy alternatives.

When Health Becomes Predictable

One of the most profound experiences reported by individuals achieving Effortless Effectiveness is predictability. Energy levels stabilize. Sleep becomes reliable. Mood fluctuations decrease. Recovery patterns become consistent. Once again, automation.

Predictability produces psychological safety. Individuals trust their body's signals. Anxiety surrounding health diminishes. Decision-making becomes clearer because biological volatility decreases.

Predictable physiology creates predictable performance. Predictable performance supports confidence and resilience across professional and personal domains.

The Long-Term Vision of Effortless Effectiveness

Effortless Effectiveness is not about reaching a static endpoint. It represents a dynamic equilibrium between adaptation and stability. As individuals age, environmental demands shift, and physiological needs evolve. Integrated habits adjust accordingly.

The goal is not to freeze the body in optimal condition indefinitely. The goal is to create adaptive resilience capable of evolving alongside life's changes.

Effortless Effectiveness prepares individuals for longevity not merely in lifespan but in functional vitality.

When Health Stops Feeling Fragile

At the beginning of most health journeys, people feel fragile. One poor meal feels catastrophic. One missed workout feels like regression. One disrupted night of sleep feels like collapse.

Effortless Effectiveness dissolves fragility. Individuals trust their baseline resilience. They recognize that temporary deviation does not destroy progress. They operate inside stable physiological systems capable of absorbing stress without collapse.

This is not complacency. It is biological confidence.

Health becomes durable. Behavior becomes intuitive. Vitality becomes sustainable.

In the next chapter, we will explore how sustained effectiveness translates into measurable output across physical performance, cognitive function, and longevity metrics, completing the final stage of optimized human vitality.

CHAPTER 13

Optimal Output

When Health Becomes Performance, Clarity, and Longevity

The Real Definition of Performance

Most people associate performance with physical strength or athletic capability. They imagine elite athletes, body composition, endurance metrics, or competitive outcomes. Performance, however, is far broader and far more meaningful than physical exertion alone.

True performance is the ability to consistently produce desired outcomes across every domain of life. It is the capacity to think clearly under pressure. It is the ability to sustain energy throughout a demanding day. It is emotional stability during adversity. It is cognitive sharpness when decisions carry significant consequences. It is physical resilience when the body faces stress, travel, or aging.

Performance is not about peak moments. It is about reliable capability.

Optimal Output represents the culmination of The AI MD™ framework. It is the stage where biological optimization translates into measurable life execution. The purpose of health is not merely to avoid disease. The purpose of health is to expand human capacity.

Why Vitality Precedes Achievement

Human achievement is often framed as a matter of intelligence, discipline, or opportunity. While these variables contribute to success, they all depend on a more foundational resource: biological energy.

Energy determines cognitive processing speed. Energy influences emotional stability. Energy controls motivation. Energy affects creativity, memory consolidation, and decision quality. When energy is compromised, every domain of performance deteriorates simultaneously.

Many individuals attempt to optimize productivity without stabilizing energy physiology. They pursue time management strategies, motivational frameworks, or cognitive enhancement protocols while ignoring sleep quality, metabolic balance, and recovery capacity. These approaches produce inconsistent results because they attempt to amplify output without strengthening the biological engine producing it.

Optimal Output begins with energy stability.

The Neurobiology of High-Level Output

The brain consumes approximately twenty percent of the body's metabolic resources despite representing a small fraction of total body mass. Cognitive performance depends heavily on glucose regulation, oxygen delivery, neurotransmitter balance, and circadian synchronization.

When metabolic variability increases, cognitive clarity declines. When sleep fragmentation occurs, executive function deteriorates. When chronic stress elevates cortisol beyond adaptive thresholds, memory and emotional regulation weaken.

Optimal Output is the product of neurological efficiency supported by systemic physiological stability. Cognitive performance cannot be separated from physical health. Emotional regulation cannot be isolated from metabolic balance. Human performance is an integrated biological phenomenon.

The Stability-Intensity Performance Curve

High achievers frequently pursue intensity. They operate in environments demanding prolonged focus, rapid decision-making, and sustained emotional regulation. Intensity can temporarily elevate performance. However, intensity without stability produces volatility.

The Stability-Intensity Performance Curve illustrates this relationship. When individuals possess stable sleep patterns, metabolic consistency, and recovery capacity, they can tolerate higher intensity without performance degradation. Without stability, increased intensity accelerates burnout, cognitive fatigue, and emotional dysregulation.

Optimal Output is not achieved by maximizing intensity. It is achieved by maximizing sustainable intensity built upon biological stability.

Emotional Regulation as a Performance Multiplier

Emotional volatility represents one of the most underestimated performance disruptors. Stress, anxiety, and mood fluctuations directly impair cognitive clarity and decision-making accuracy. Emotional dysregulation reduces interpersonal effectiveness and increases impulsive behavior patterns.

Physiological metrics such as HRV provide insight into autonomic nervous system balance. Higher HRV often correlates with improved emotional adaptability. Stable HRV trends indicate improved parasympathetic activation, supporting stress recovery and cognitive resilience.

Optimal Output requires emotional regulation not as a psychological luxury but as a biological necessity. Individuals who stabilize autonomic nervous system balance gain significant performance advantages across professional, relational, and creative domains.

The Cognitive Economy of Biological Optimization

Every cognitive process carries metabolic cost. Decision-making, problem-solving, and creative thinking consume glucose and oxygen while generating neurological fatigue. When individuals experience unstable blood glucose levels or inadequate oxygenation due to poor sleep or cardiovascular inefficiency, cognitive endurance declines rapidly.

Optimal Output conserves cognitive energy through biological optimization. Stable glucose availability supports sustained concentration. Efficient cardiovascular function improves oxygen delivery to neural tissue. Deep sleep enhances synaptic pruning and memory consolidation, preparing the brain for subsequent learning cycles.

Cognitive brilliance is not purely intellectual. It is metabolic.

Longevity as Sustained Output Potential

Longevity is frequently misunderstood as extended lifespan. Within The AI MD™ framework, longevity represents extended performance capacity. Living longer carries limited value if vitality deteriorates during those additional years.

Optimal Output aligns lifespan with healthspan. It emphasizes preserving muscular strength, cognitive sharpness, metabolic flexibility, and emotional stability across decades. Preventing chronic disease becomes secondary to maintaining high-level functional capability.

Longevity-focused performance integrates cardiovascular health, metabolic resilience, neurological preservation, and musculoskeletal integrity. These systems collectively determine whether extended lifespan translates into sustained productivity and fulfillment.

Case Study: Entrepreneurial Cognitive Longevity

A technology entrepreneur experienced progressive cognitive fatigue during rapid company expansion. Despite maintaining exercise routines and nutritional awareness, sleep variability and chronic stress disrupted recovery patterns. Cognitive performance fluctuated dramatically, impairing strategic decision-making.

Through The AI MD™ framework and implementation, sleep consistency became the primary intervention. Continuous monitoring revealed fragmented sleep architecture despite adequate total sleep duration. Environmental modifications and circadian stabilization improved sleep efficiency. The power to know thyself and break down details of your sleep is transformative. Leveraging this information to make the necessary adjustments will lead to your own high-level output. In this case study, HRV trends stabilized within weeks which correlated with improved emotional regulation and cognitive clarity.

The entrepreneur reported enhanced strategic thinking, improved conflict resolution, and sustained focus during extended work cycles. Revenue growth accelerated not because of increased working hours but because of improved cognitive quality during decision-making windows.

Optimal Output enhances leadership effectiveness by optimizing biological function. Having this level of insight into your own thinking and making sleep architecture adjustments can be transformative. Connecting the dots between your own insights, feelings and wearable data allows for such outcome driven strategic actions.

The Relationship Between Physical Strength and Cognitive Power

Muscular strength correlates with cognitive preservation and metabolic resilience. Resistance training stimulates hormonal responses supporting neuroplasticity and insulin sensitivity. Increased muscular mass enhances glucose storage capacity, stabilizing energy availability for neurological function.

Physical strength also improves injury resistance, enabling consistent activity participation. Movement consistency reinforces cardiovascular conditioning and mitochondrial density, supporting cellular energy production.

Optimal Output integrates strength training not as aesthetic pursuit but as neurological and metabolic performance enhancement.

The Cardiovascular Foundation of Output

Cardiovascular efficiency determines oxygen transport capacity throughout the body. Improved oxygen delivery enhances mitochondrial ATP production, supporting muscular endurance and cognitive processing.

VO_2 max, a measure of maximal oxygen utilization, correlates strongly with longevity and overall performance capacity. Individuals with higher cardiovascular efficiency demonstrate superior endurance, improved recovery rates, and reduced chronic disease risk.

Optimal Output requires integrating cardiovascular conditioning as foundational infrastructure supporting systemic performance.

Metabolic Flexibility and Performance Adaptability

Metabolic flexibility refers to the body's ability to transition efficiently between carbohydrate and fat metabolism depending on activity demands. Individuals with poor metabolic flexibility experience energy crashes, cognitive fatigue, and inconsistent physical performance.

Optimizing metabolic flexibility through nutritional periodization, exercise variability, and circadian alignment stabilizes energy availability across diverse physiological demands.

Optimal Output emerges when energy systems adapt seamlessly to cognitive, emotional, and physical challenges without significant performance degradation.

The Psychological Confidence of Biological Reliability

Consistent biological performance creates psychological confidence. Individuals trust their energy levels, cognitive clarity, and emotional stability. Confidence reduces anxiety associated with unpredictable performance fluctuations. Decision-making becomes more decisive. Leadership presence strengthens. Creativity expands without fear of cognitive collapse.

Biological reliability transforms self-perception. Individuals transition from managing limitations to expressing capability.

The AI MD™ Performance Integration Model

Optimal Output integrates four core physiological pillars:

1. Neurological efficiency supports cognitive clarity and emotional regulation.
2. Metabolic stability sustains energy availability and hormonal balance.

3. Cardiovascular conditioning enhances endurance and oxygen delivery.
4. Musculoskeletal strength preserves mobility, injury resistance, and metabolic support.

These pillars interact continuously. Weakness within any domain compromises overall performance potential. Strength across all domains produces multiplicative performance enhancement rather than additive improvement. Your body is more interconnected than you might realize. This is a core reason why HRV gives us insights into other elements of physiological pillars.

Technology as Performance Amplification

Wearable technology supports Optimal Output through early detection of performance degradation signals. HRV trends identify stress overload before symptomatic burnout occurs. Sleep staging reveals recovery deficiencies impacting cognitive output. Continuous metabolic monitoring identifies nutritional patterns impairing energy stability.

Technology provides performance intelligence. It identifies drift before functional decline becomes visible. Proper interpretation allows proactive adjustment preserving high-level output.

The Performance Cost of Chronic Stress

Chronic stress disrupts hormonal balance, increases inflammatory markers, and impairs immune resilience. Elevated cortisol levels impair memory formation and reduce neuroplasticity. Chronic sympathetic activation decreases HRV and emotional adaptability.

Optimal Output requires structured stress management integrating physiological recovery protocols. Breathwork, recovery training, circadian regulation, and emotional processing techniques restore autonomic balance. Stress management becomes performance optimization rather than relaxation indulgence.

Output Sustainability Across Life Phases

Human performance requirements evolve across life stages. Early adulthood emphasizes physical strength and cognitive acquisition. Midlife performance prioritizes strategic thinking, emotional intelligence, and leadership stability. Later-life performance emphasizes wisdom integration and physiological preservation.

Optimal Output adapts health strategies to life phase demands. Training intensity, recovery protocols, and cognitive stimulation evolve with aging physiology. The objective remains consistent: preserving functional capability aligned with personal and professional goals.

The AI MD™ Principle:
Health exists to expand human capability.

Health is not a defensive strategy against disease. It is an offensive strategy for capability expansion. Optimal Output occurs when biological systems operate efficiently enough to support sustained intellectual, emotional, and physical achievement.

Performance becomes predictable. Productivity becomes reliable. Creativity becomes sustainable.

The Cultural Shift Toward Performance Medicine

Traditional medicine focuses primarily on disease diagnosis and treatment. Performance medicine expands the clinical mission toward optimizing functional capacity before disease emerges. AI-assisted monitoring enables early detection of physiological drift and supports personalized intervention strategies.

Optimal Output represents the philosophical evolution of healthcare. Medicine transitions from reactive disease management to proactive human optimization.

The Measurement of True Output

True output cannot be measured solely through productivity metrics. It includes quality of relationships, creative contribution, emotional resilience, and long-term vitality. Quantitative metrics must be interpreted alongside qualitative life satisfaction indicators.

Optimal Output integrates both dimensions. It recognizes that peak performance loses meaning if it sacrifices relational fulfillment or psychological well-being. Sustainable output requires holistic balance.

The Legacy of Biological Optimization

Individuals achieving Optimal Output influence their families, organizations, and communities. Biological optimization enhances leadership presence, decision accuracy, and emotional stability. These traits propagate through professional environments and personal relationships. They create generational performance influence.

Health becomes *legacy* infrastructure rather than individual achievement. Imagine this level of achievement. You cannot buy your way to it, it can only be achieved! AI and wearables will get you there.

When Capacity Becomes Identity

Optimal Output represents the moment when individuals stop asking whether they can perform at high levels. They begin assuming capability as baseline identity. Biological stability removes internal barriers to expression. Talent, intelligence, and creativity emerge without physiological interference.

This is not perfection. It is reliability.

Health becomes invisible infrastructure supporting visible achievement.

In the final chapter, we will translate Optimal Output into actionable execution strategies, providing structured pathways for sustaining The AI MD™ methodology across daily life implementation and long-term transformation.

CHAPTER 14

Prescribed Practice

The Results Execution Plan

The Moment Where Knowledge Becomes Action

Every system eventually faces its most important test. Not whether it is intelligent. Not whether it is clinically sound. Not whether it is innovative or technologically advanced. The ultimate test is whether it changes behavior.

Knowledge alone does not produce transformation. Awareness alone does not produce results. Even motivation, as powerful as it feels in the moment, rarely produces lasting change without structure.

Prescribed Practice exists because understanding health optimization is fundamentally different from living it.

This chapter is where theory becomes rhythm. Where insight becomes implementation. Where potential becomes consistency.

The AI MD™ framework was never designed to be inspirational alone. It was built to be executable.

Why Most Health Improvements Fail After Good Intentions

One of the most common patterns observed in clinical medicine and personal health improvement is the enthusiasm cycle. Individuals experience a moment of realization, often triggered by a diagnosis, a medical scare, a major life transition, or exposure to new information. That realization produces urgency. Urgency produces immediate behavioral change. The change produces temporary results.

Then something predictable happens.

Life resumes its complexity. Responsibilities return. Emotional stressors reappear. Time becomes scarce. The new behavior begins competing with existing routines, and slowly, almost invisibly, the improvement fades.

This failure rarely occurs because individuals lack discipline or desire. The failure occurs because the new behavior was never structurally integrated into daily life. It existed as an effort, not as a system. It was not automatic.

Prescribed Practice transforms health optimization from effort into infrastructure.

The Difference Between Effort and Infrastructure

Effort requires conscious motivation every time an action is performed. Infrastructure makes the action automatic because it is built into environmental, psychological, and biological rhythms.

Brushing your teeth does not require motivation because it is infrastructure. Checking your phone in the morning does not require motivation because it is infrastructure. Your commute route does not require daily decision-making because it is infrastructure.

Health transformation must reach this same level of integration if it is going to produce durable results.

Prescribed Practice is the process of building biological infrastructure.

The Rhythm Model of Health Execution

The AI MD™ implementation framework is built around biological rhythm rather than behavioral pressure. The human body operates through cycles. Circadian rhythm governs hormonal secretion. Ultradian rhythm governs cognitive performance cycles. Sleep cycles govern neurological restoration. Metabolic rhythm governs energy utilization and storage.

Prescribed Practice aligns health behaviors with biological timing rather than forcing behaviors through willpower alone.

When health behaviors synchronize with natural physiological cycles, compliance increases dramatically while perceived effort decreases.

The Three Tiers of Prescribed Practice

Prescribed Practice operates through three implementation tiers. Each tier represents a different time scale of execution.

1. Daily micro practices maintain biological stability.
2. Weekly calibration practices adjust behavioral direction.
3. Quarterly strategic reviews refine long-term optimization strategy.

These tiers create layered consistency. They ensure that small daily actions align with larger physiological and performance objectives.

Tier 1: Daily Micro Practices

Daily Micro Practices are the smallest repeatable actions that protect biological stability. Their purpose is not dramatic transformation. Their purpose is preventing drift.

Sleep anchoring represents the most critical daily micro practice. Consistent sleep and wake windows stabilize circadian hormone release, regulate cortisol rhythms, and enhance metabolic efficiency. Even minor improvements in sleep timing consistency produce measurable improvements in cognitive clarity, emotional regulation, and recovery capacity.

Movement exposure represents the second foundational daily micro practice. Human physiology evolved under regular movement patterns. Sedentary behavior disrupts insulin sensitivity, cardiovascular conditioning, and musculoskeletal integrity. Prescribed Practice recommends consistent daily movement exposure, even on non-training days, to maintain metabolic and neurological stimulation.

Hydration consistency supports cardiovascular function, thermoregulation, and cognitive performance. Even mild dehydration can impair concentration and physical endurance. Structured hydration timing integrated into daily routine reduces variability in physiological performance.

Nutritional rhythm stabilizes glucose availability and hormonal signaling. Prescribed Practice emphasizes consistent meal timing aligned with activity demand and circadian metabolic sensitivity.

These micro practices operate as baseline maintenance. They protect biological systems from destabilization.

Tier 2: Weekly Calibration Practices

Weekly calibration introduces reflective evaluation. It allows individuals to interpret biometric trends and behavioral responses over meaningful timeframes rather than reacting to daily variability.

Weekly HRV and sleep trend evaluation provides insight into stress load accumulation and recovery adequacy. Weekly exercise performance evaluation identifies adaptation progress or overtraining risk. Weekly nutritional adherence reflection evaluates metabolic consistency.

Weekly calibration prevents overreaction to temporary fluctuations while allowing early detection of systemic drift.

It also reinforces accountability without creating psychological pressure associated with daily score interpretation.

Tier 3: Quarterly Strategic Reviews

Biological transformation occurs across extended time horizons. Quarterly Strategic Reviews allow recalibration of health priorities based on changing performance demands, life circumstances, and physiological adaptation.

Quarterly reviews assess changes in strength capacity, cardiovascular conditioning, metabolic markers, and cognitive performance sustainability. They evaluate whether interventions remain aligned with evolving goals.

Prescribed Practice recognizes that health optimization is dynamic. Static protocols eventually become ineffective because human physiology continuously adapts.

The Minimum Effective Dose Philosophy

Many individuals attempt to implement health optimization through maximal effort strategies. They attempt simultaneous dietary overhauls, aggressive training programs, supplement expansion, and rigid behavioral rules.

This approach produces initial enthusiasm followed by rapid burnout.

Prescribed Practice operates through the Minimum Effective Dose philosophy. It identifies the smallest consistent behavior capable of producing meaningful physiological adaptation. The objective is sustainability, not intensity.

Small, repeatable actions accumulate into major transformation when executed with precision and consistency.

Environmental Engineering for Health Consistency

Behavioral science consistently demonstrates that environment shapes behavior more reliably than motivation. Prescribed Practice integrates environmental engineering strategies to support health execution.

Sleep environment optimization includes temperature regulation, light exposure management, and electronic device boundaries. Nutritional environment design includes food availability planning and decision fatigue reduction. Movement environment design includes visible exercise equipment placement and schedule integration.

Environmental design reduces reliance on moment-to-moment willpower. It allows biological infrastructure to operate through default behavioral pathways.

The Psychological Contract of Prescribed Practice

Long-term health optimization requires redefining personal identity. Individuals must transition from viewing health behaviors as obligations to viewing them as non-negotiable components of self-expression.

Prescribed Practice establishes a psychological contract. Individuals commit not to perfection, but to continuity. Missing a single practice does not represent failure. Abandoning rhythm represents failure.

Continuity creates identity reinforcement. Identity reinforcement strengthens behavioral persistence. Everything comes back to the long game. Small adjustments have big impacts over time on your health. This concept is well established in finance, but I have always felt it is less emphasized in personal health. The solution would be to visualize how small changes can create meaningful impacts with the use of a biosimulator. More on biosimulation in the final chapter.

The Role of AI in Execution Accountability

AI integration enhances Prescribed Practice by identifying subtle pattern changes before individuals consciously recognize them. Machine learning algorithms detect HRV drift, sleep variability, metabolic irregularity, and training load imbalance earlier than subjective awareness typically allows.

AI does not replace human accountability. It strengthens awareness precision. It transforms biometric monitoring into early warning intelligence.

Execution improves when individuals respond to predictive insight rather than reactive symptom management.

Prescribed Recovery as Performance Strategy

Recovery is frequently misunderstood as inactivity. Prescribed Practice reframes recovery as active physiological restoration.

Sleep depth optimization enhances growth hormone secretion and memory consolidation. Active recovery movement enhances lymphatic circulation and muscular repair. Parasympathetic stimulation practices enhance autonomic balance and stress resilience.

Recovery becomes a strategic performance multiplier rather than a passive rest period.

The Social Dimension of Execution

Human behavior is strongly influenced by social context. Prescribed Practice incorporates accountability partnerships, coaching structures, or community integration when appropriate.

Social reinforcement increases adherence probability and provides psychological support during adaptation phases. Behavioral sustainability improves when individuals feel supported rather than isolated.

Failure Protocols and Behavioral Reset

Every implementation system must include failure protocols. Prescribed Practice assumes behavioral disruption will occur during travel, illness, stress, or life transition periods.

Failure protocols focus on rapid re-entry rather than self-criticism. Individuals identify the smallest reactivation behavior capable of restoring rhythm. This may involve sleep stabilization, hydration restoration, or simplified movement reintroduction.

Rapid re-entry prevents temporary disruption from becoming permanent regression. At the end of the day, consistency is what matters. You are allowed to create failure protocols as inevitably life will happen.

The AI MD™ Principle:
Consistency outperforms intensity.

High intensity produces temporary transformation. Consistency produces permanent transformation. Prescribed Practice prioritizes behavioral repeatability over behavioral magnitude.

Small improvements executed continuously outperform aggressive interventions executed inconsistently.

The Emotional Resistance to Structured Living

Some individuals resist Prescribed Practice because structure feels restrictive. They fear losing spontaneity or lifestyle flexibility. In reality, structured biological rhythm increases freedom.

When energy becomes predictable, individuals gain freedom to pursue creativity, leadership, and personal relationships without physiological limitation. Structure does not eliminate spontaneity, it supports it.

The Physician's Perspective on Compliance Reality

Clinical medicine consistently demonstrates that treatment effectiveness depends more heavily on compliance than prescription accuracy. My favorite clinical case on compliance and prescription accuracy is a patient who kept coming into the clinic with an elevated blood pressure. Each time he would come for a visit, his blood pressure was high. My colleague kept increasing the dose of his blood pressure medicine to no avail. When my colleague asked my thoughts on pursuing a secondary high blood pressure work up, I simply asked him if he really checked to see that the patient was even taking the medication. Turns out the patient was too embarrassed to admit to his doctor that he was not taking his medications. The lack of compliance negated any prescription accuracy.

Even perfectly designed interventions fail when they cannot be integrated into daily life and routines.

Prescribed Practice prioritizes compliance design. It ensures that interventions fit realistically within professional, familial, desired, and social obligations.

Health optimization succeeds when it respects human complexity.

Long-Term Execution and Aging Physiology

Prescribed Practice evolves across lifespan stages. Early adulthood emphasizes building physiological reserve capacity. Midlife execution emphasizes maintaining resilience under cumulative stress. Later life execution emphasizes preserving independence and cognitive longevity.

The AI MD™ execution model adapts intervention emphasis based on physiological aging patterns. Health strategy remains dynamic rather than static.

The Legacy Effect of Execution Discipline

Individuals who successfully implement Prescribed Practice influence family health culture and organizational wellness culture. Behavioral modeling propagates across generations and professional communities.

Execution discipline becomes legacy transmission.

The AI MD™ Daily Execution Blueprint

While individual prescriptions vary, Prescribed Practice typically includes:

- Morning circadian activation through light exposure and hydration.
- Midday metabolic stability through structured nutritional timing and movement breaks.
- Evening nervous system downregulation through screen reduction and recovery preparation.

These anchor points stabilize biological rhythm across daily cycles.

The Relationship Between Simplicity and Sustainability

Complex health routines often create compliance failure. Prescribed Practice intentionally favors simplicity. Simplicity enhances adherence probability and reduces psychological friction.

Effective health infrastructure should feel sustainable rather than overwhelming.

Prescribed Practice as Identity Integration

Long-term transformation occurs when health behaviors transition from scheduled tasks to identity expressions. Individuals stop asking whether they should execute health behaviors. They begin assuming those behaviors reflect who they are.

Identity integration represents the final stage of behavioral permanence.

The System That Protects Your Future Self

Prescribed Practice is not designed for your present motivation. It is designed for your future unpredictability. There will be seasons where stress increases, time compresses, or life complexity expands.

Infrastructure protects consistency when motivation disappears.

Health optimization becomes resilient when it survives emotional variability, professional pressure, and environmental disruption.

Prescribed Practice ensures that The AI MD™ system becomes a living rhythm rather than a temporary improvement phase.

Transition Toward Final Integration

You have now traveled through the full methodology of The AI MD™. You have learned how to interpret data, align biological systems, activate corrective strategy, and implement execution rhythm.

The final step is not another system. It is a decision.

In the epilogue, we step beyond methodology into invitation. An invitation to commit to personal health leadership, professional integration, and lifelong biological optimization.

Because ultimately, The AI MD™ method is not a program. It is a paradigm.

EPILOGUE

The End of Guessing

From Data to Destiny

The Quiet Truth Most People Already Know

If you've read this far, you probably already feel it.

Not intellectually. Not academically. But somewhere deeper than analysis.

You feel the quiet truth that something about modern health has been incomplete. You've likely sensed that the abundance of information hasn't produced the clarity it promised. That more tracking hasn't always created more confidence. Sometimes, the more you learned, the more uncertain you became.

You are not alone in that experience.

For years, healthcare has operated inside a paradox. We have developed extraordinary diagnostic tools, revolutionary treatments, and unprecedented access to data. Yet many individuals feel more disconnected from their health than ever before. They have numbers but not direction. Metrics but not meaning. Monitoring but not mastery.

This book was written to resolve that paradox.

Not by replacing science. Not by dismissing technology. Not by pretending complexity doesn't exist. But by restoring order to the way we interpret the human body.

The Purpose Behind The AI MD™ Method

The AI MD™ method was built on a simple but powerful belief.

Your health should not feel like guesswork.

Every chapter you've read was designed to remove one layer of confusion that modern health culture has normalized. You've learned how data can mislead when it lacks intention. You've learned how technology can overwhelm when it lacks hierarchy. You've learned how optimization fails when it lacks execution rhythm.

Most importantly, you've learned that your body is not a random collection of metrics. It is an integrated biological system capable of remarkable adaptation when guided correctly.

The AI MD™ framework was never meant to give you more information. It was built to give you interpretation. It was built to help you transition from passive health monitoring into active health leadership.

Because there is a fundamental difference between knowing your data and understanding your direction.

The Three Decisions Every Reader Must Make

At this point in the journey, information alone is no longer the question. The only question that remains is decision.

Every individual who encounters meaningful health insight eventually arrives at three crossroads.

1. The first decision is whether to remain reactive or become intentional. Reactive health waits for symptoms, lab abnormalities, or crises to create urgency. Intentional health defines outcomes before problems emerge. *Prevention > Reaction.*

2. The second decision is whether to remain fragmented or become integrated. Fragmented health separates sleep from stress, nutrition from metabolism, performance from recovery. Integrated health recognizes that biological systems operate as a network, not as isolated functions.
3. The third decision is whether to remain temporary or become consistent. Temporary health improvement relies on motivation spikes. Consistent health improvement relies on structured rhythm.

These decisions are not made once. They are made repeatedly through daily execution.

Why Clarity Creates Relief Before Results Appear

One of the most remarkable observations in clinical medicine is how frequently patients experience emotional relief the moment a clear diagnostic plan is established, even before treatment begins.

The same phenomenon exists in personal health transformation.

When individuals finally understand what they are solving, how they will measure it, and what steps will follow, uncertainty decreases dramatically. Anxiety decreases. Confidence increases. Direction replaces confusion.

Clarity reduces psychological stress before physiological change even occurs.

This is not accidental. The human nervous system seeks predictability. When direction becomes visible, the brain transitions from threat mode into planning mode. That shift alone improves cognitive function, emotional resilience, and behavioral compliance.

The AI MD™ method is designed to create that clarity.

The Escalator and The Elevator

There are two ways individuals and professionals typically engage with health transformation. I describe them metaphorically as the escalator and the elevator.

The escalator represents gradual, self-paced implementation. Individuals who choose the escalator absorb information, apply foundational practices, refine routines, and progress through steady self-guided improvement. The escalator is reliable, sustainable, and entirely valid. Many people achieve extraordinary health transformation through disciplined personal implementation.

The elevator represents accelerated, professionally guided integration. Individuals or clinicians who choose the elevator move rapidly through structured coaching, advanced biometric analysis, clinical consultation, or professional certification. The elevator provides speed, precision, and direct mentorship. It compresses learning curves and allows for more complex intervention strategies.

Neither path is superior. They simply serve different readiness levels, professional goals, and personal timelines.

What matters most is choosing movement rather than remaining stationary.

For The Individual Reader

If you are reading this as someone seeking to improve your own health, your next step is not complicated. It is not overwhelming. It is not dependent on purchasing additional technology or enrolling in complex programs.

Your next step is execution.

Define one clear outcome. Establish your Baseline Health Indicator. Begin Prescribed Practice. Focus on consistency rather than perfection. Allow your biological rhythm to stabilize. Allow your interpretation of data to mature over time.

Health transformation rarely occurs through dramatic overnight change. It occurs through stable, repeatable behaviors executed long enough for physiology to adapt.

Your body is remarkably responsive when given consistent instruction.

For The Clinician, Coach, or Health Professional

If you are reading this as a practitioner, your invitation carries additional responsibility.

Healthcare to some degree has always been in a transformation era. Artificial intelligence, wearable technology, remote monitoring, and predictive modeling are expanding the way patient care is delivered. These tools offer extraordinary opportunity but also introduce unprecedented complexity.

Patients do not simply need more data. They need translation. They need integration. They need professionals capable of guiding interpretation and designing execution frameworks.

The AI MD™ methodology exists to support that evolution. It provides clinicians, coaches, and wellness professionals with a structured model to integrate biometric intelligence into patient-centered care.

If you choose to adopt this framework professionally, you become part of a movement redefining preventive medicine, performance optimization, and personalized health leadership.

The Responsibility That Comes With Awareness

Once individuals understand the relationship between data and destiny, something changes. Health becomes less accidental. Outcomes become less random. Personal responsibility increases.

This responsibility is not meant to feel heavy. It is meant to feel empowering. You gain the ability to influence your longevity, performance capacity, emotional resilience, and cognitive clarity in ways previous generations could only imagine.

You are living during the first era in human history where predictive biometric insight is accessible to the general population. That access carries opportunity and responsibility simultaneously.

The AI MD™ framework exists to help you navigate both.

Why The Future of Health Will Be Predictive, Personalized, and Participatory

The healthcare model of the future will not revolve around episodic crisis treatment alone. It will revolve around predictive monitoring, personalized intervention design, and active patient participation.

Predictive health identifies risk patterns before symptoms appear. Personalized health designs interventions based on individual physiology rather than population averages. Participatory health empowers individuals to become active collaborators in their care rather than passive recipients.

This transformation requires new literacy. It requires individuals and professionals who understand how to interpret and apply biometric intelligence responsibly.

This book represents an introduction to that literacy.

The Legacy of Consistent Execution

Health is rarely an isolated personal experience. Behavioral patterns influence families, workplaces, communities, and future generations. Children observe parental health habits. Teams observe leadership energy and resilience. Social networks replicate behavioral norms.

Consistent health execution creates generational ripple effects.

When individuals stabilize their energy, improve cognitive clarity, and maintain physical resilience, they influence everyone within their relational orbit. Health optimization becomes a leadership practice.

The AI MD™ Principle:
The goal is not perfect health. The goal is predictable direction.

Perfect health is an illusion. Predictable direction is achievable. When individuals maintain stable biological rhythm, early warning patterns become visible. Minor adjustments prevent major crises. Adaptation becomes continuous rather than reactive.

Predictable direction produces longevity, performance sustainability, and emotional stability.

The Commitment Moment

Every meaningful transformation contains a moment where information transitions into commitment. That moment does not occur through external pressure. It occurs through internal decisions.

This is that moment.

You now understand how to assess your health intelligently. You understand how to align biological systems with intention. You understand how to activate corrective strategies and implement Prescribed Practice.

The only remaining step is choosing whether you will live this knowledge or simply admire it.

A Personal Reflection

As a physician, I have spent years watching patients navigate fear, uncertainty, diagnosis, recovery, and resilience. I have witnessed extraordinary recovery stories and devastating preventable outcomes. I have learned that the difference between those two paths often begins long before disease appears.

It begins with awareness. It begins with interpretation. It begins with decision.

The AI MD™ method was created because I believe individuals deserve clarity earlier in their health journey. They deserve guidance before crisis. They deserve tools that empower rather than overwhelm.

This book represents that belief.

The Invitation Forward

You now have two invitations.

The first invitation is personal. Continue your health journey using The AI MD™ method as your execution framework. Apply the principles consistently. Refine them as your life evolves. Allow your biology to respond to structured leadership. Learn more about the Biosimulator I created to help you visualize how small changes make big impacts on disease states. Visualizing adjustments to your HRV with my biosimulator can really open your eyes to the power of small changes. This will hopefully convince you it is all about the long game when it comes to your health. Short term setbacks should never derail you again. When you visit my website (https://theaimd.ai) for more information, you can sync your wearable to give you personalized biosimulation of potential future health outcomes. If the outcomes are not desired, simply reverse engineer a preventative strategy and demonstrate to yourself what adjustments need to be made to achieve your desirable results. Beyond biosimulation, allowing AI to guide you without the hypervigilant data and decision making will move you towards a path of Effortless Effectiveness.

The second invitation is professional. If you are a clinician, coach, or health leader who believes in the future of predictive and personalized medicine, you are invited to explore deeper integration of this methodology within your practice or professional development. There is an ocean of opportunity for clinicians to serve their own patient populations and communities. Serving people better to optimize their health now requires the use of wearables and wearable insights.

Both invitations lead to intentional health optimization as a forever event.

The End of Guessing

Guessing creates anxiety. Guessing creates inconsistency. Guessing creates delayed intervention and missed opportunity.

Clarity creates calm. Clarity creates direction. Clarity creates transformation.

You no longer need to guess.

You now understand how to translate data into meaning. You understand how to convert insight into rhythm. You understand how to guide your biology toward sustainable performance and longevity.

Your health journey will still require effort. It will still require patience. It will still require adaptation. But it no longer has to require uncertainty.

The Final Thought

Your body has always been communicating with you. Technology has simply given that communication translatability. The AI MD™ method teaches you how to listen, interpret, and respond.

Health is not a destination you reach once. It is a relationship you maintain continuously.

Relationships, when guided with clarity, consistency, and intention, become stronger over time.

This is not the end of your health journey.

This is the end of guessing.

Glossary of Terms

Active Recovery Movement: low-intensity physical activity performed between harder training sessions to promote circulation and muscle repair without adding stress.

Adaptive Refinement: process by which a person continuously improves their approach based on feedback and results over time.

The AI MD™ Method: a physician-led framework for using AI and wearables to improve health decisions moving from noise to knowledge, and knowledge to action.

Alert Fatigue: phenomenon that happens when you have received so many notifications, warnings, and alerts.

Almost Syndrome: the frustrating state of being almost healthy, almost optimized, and almost at your goal.

Anticoagulated: medical state in which blood-thinning medication has been used to reduce the body's ability to clot.

Artificial Clarity: the false sense of understanding or certainty that comes from having too much data.

Artificial Confusion: the overwhelm and uncertainty created when technology generates more information than you can meaningfully interpret or act on.

Baseline Code: your body's unique biological fingerprint that is based on health metrics, and patterns that define what normal looks like for you.

Baseline Health Indicator: your personal normal that is set based on activity, heart rate variability, and sleep.

Baroreflex Sensitivity: your body's ability to quickly detect and correct changes in blood pressure.

Bioadaptive Behavior: practice of consciously adjusting your daily habits and choices in direct response to what your body's data is telling you in real time.

Biosimulation: the use of computational models to simulate clinical outcomes based on your own personal health data.

Cardiovascular Efficiency: the ability of the heart and circulatory system to deliver oxygen and nutrients throughout the body with minimal effort.

Circadian Alignment: state in which your daily behaviors are timed in sync with your body's internal biological clock.

Circadian Synchronization: active process of coordinating your lifestyle habits with your circadian rhythm to optimize energy, mood, metabolism, and recovery.

Clinical Informatics: the field of medicine for which the science of using data and technology are leveraged to provide decision support to make healthcare more effective/efficient.

Corrective Adaptation: the process of adjusting behavior in response to physiological feedback.

Dynamic Calibration: continuous, real-time adjustment of targets based on continuously updated data from your own body.

Dysmorphia: distorted or inaccurate perception of one's own body or appearance.

ECG: electrocardiogram – a test that records electrical activity of the heart.

Feedback Fog: state of confusion that sets in when you are receiving so many health signals, scores, and recommendations from so many different sources that none of them register clearly enough to act on.

Effortless Effectiveness: a state in which healthy habits have become so well established that optimal choices require little conscious effort or willpower.

Genomic: complete set of DNA which contains the inherited blueprint that influences your health, traits, and disease risk.

Glucose Variability: how much your blood sugar rises and falls throughout the day.

Habit Automation: process by which repeated behaviors become automatic requiring minimal mental energy as they are hardwired into your routine.

Health Dysmorphia: distorted perception of one's own health.

Heart Rate Variability: variations in time between each heartbeat.

Hypertrophy: growth and enlargement of muscle tissue that occurs in response to resistance training and physical stress.

Hypoxic: a state of low oxygen.

Infinite Insight: paradoxical state of having unlimited access to health data and analysis.

Informatics: the science of collecting, organizing, and making sense of information so it can be used more effectively.

Insomnia: difficulty with falling or staying asleep.

Intelligent Integration: thoughtful incorporation of data, tools, or technologies into daily life in a way that enhances rather than complicates well-being.

Interoception: your body's ability to sense and interpret its own internal signals.

Metabolic Disease: group of conditions where the body's ability to produce, store or use energy is disrupted. Examples include diabetes, high cholesterol, and obesity.

Metabolic Flexibility: the body's ability to efficiently switch between burning carbohydrates and fat for fuel depending on availability and need.

Metrics Mirage: illusion of health progress created by improving numbers that do not tell the whole story.

Number Dysmorphia: fixation on health metrics to the point where the numbers drive anxiety rather than insight.

Nutritional Periodization: strategic adjustment of food intake to match the demands of different training phases.

Optimal Output: level of performance, productivity, or physical output that is both peak and sustainable.

Optimization Fatigue: exhaustion that sets in when the constant effort to improve, track, and perfect every aspect of your health stops feeling empowering and starts feeling like a burden.

Optimization Obsession: unhealthy fixation on maximizing every health metric where the pursuit of perfection undermines the sustainability or enjoyment of healthy living.

Optimized Overwhelm: the unintended consequence of having access to more health data than your mind and body know what to do with.

Oxygen Saturation: a measurement of how much oxygen your blood is carrying.

Paradox of Optimization: ironic reality that the relentless pursuit of peak health can itself become a source of stress, anxiety, and poor health.

Parasympathetic Stimulation Practices: intentional activities that activate your body's rest and digest system to reduce stress and promote recovery.

Pathologic: related to or caused by disease.

Performance Metrics: numbers that measure what your body can do right now.

Physiological Coherence: a state in which the heart, brain, and nervous system are working in a smooth synchronized harmony (associated with lower stress and improved mental clarity).

Physiological Load: total physical and biological stress placed on your body.

Physiological Readiness: real-time snapshot of how recovered, resilient, and resourced your body is on any given day based on recovery, sleep, and stress markers.

Physiological Strain: internal stress response your body experiences in reaction to physical or environmental demands.

Post Prandial Spikes: rise in blood sugar that occurs after eating.

Prescribed Practice: structured, intentional routine or habit that is tailored to a specific health or performance goal.

Progress Metrics: numbers that measure how your body is changing over time.

Proteomic: complete set of proteins produced by your body that reflects how your genes are being expressed.

Pulse Ox: estimation of the percentage of oxygen in your blood.

Readiness: daily snapshot of how prepared your body is to take on the day.

Recovery Index: a metric that tracks how quickly your heart rate settles down and stabilizes once you fall asleep.

Recovery Time: the time your body needs to bounce back after exercise, stress, or illness.

Sleep Architecture: the structured stages your body cycles through during sleep.

Sleep Depth Optimization: the deliberate use of lifestyle, behavioral, or environmental strategies to increase the proportion of restorative deep and REM sleep each night.

Sleep Efficiency: measure of how much of your time in bed you are actually asleep.

Sleep Onset Latency: the amount of time it takes you to fall asleep.

Solution Stack: personalized combination of tools, technologies, habits, and practices that work together to support your health and performance goals.

Somatization: emotional or psychological stress showing up as real physical symptoms with no underlying medical cause.

Stability-Intensity Performance Curve: the relationship between physiological stability and the intensity of effort.

Strain Score: a numeric value that captures how hard your body worked during the day or a workout.

Synapse Pruning: the brain's natural process of eliminating unused neural connections to improve efficiency.

Ultradian Rhythm: natural biological cycles shorter than 24 hours that govern fluctuations in alertness, focus, and energy throughout the day.

Vagal Activity: activity of the vagus nerve, which is your body's main calming signal that lowers your heart rate, promotes relaxation, and aids in digestion.

Vascular Tone: degree of tension or relaxation in the walls of blood vessels, which influences blood pressure and circulation.

VO_2: a measure of how much oxygen your body is able to use during physical activity.

VO_2 Max: maximum rate at which your body can consume oxygen during intense exercise.

APPENDIX

The AI MD™ Principles

1. When measurement becomes your morning routine, momentum won't survive your afternoon.
2. Data without context breeds fear; context without discipline breeds drift.
3. Measure less. Interpret more.
4. If perfection is the plan, dysmorphia is the destination.
5. If you can't rest without a score, the score owns you.
6. Your body is your best wearable.
7. Coherence is almost always created by subtraction.
8. Pick one intention. Let data orbit it.
9. Mental margin is medicine.
10. The goal is not to need fewer tools; it's to rely on them less.
11. Simplify the system. Understand the right things deeply.
12. If you don't define success, your wearable will define failure.
13. Your wearable can measure parts of your biology. It cannot measure your life.
14. If measurement becomes your identity, fluctuation becomes fear.
15. A metric without context is a misunderstanding waiting to happen.
16. Biological data without context is information. Biological data with context becomes insight.
17. Tracking everything does not create mastery. Tracking the right things creates clarity.
18. Baseline before breakthrough.
19. Insight creates possibility. Integration creates reality.
20. Sustainability is superior to intensity.
21. Health exists to expand human capability.
22. Consistency outperforms intensity.
23. The goal is not perfect health. The goal is predictable direction.

www.ingramcontent.com/pod-product-compliance
Lightning Source LLC
LaVergne TN
LVHW022035200926
848481LV00003B/699